Thinking about Truth

The theory of knowledge

Arguing effectively

What is truth?

Elicia Lewis

RMEP

First published in 2008 by RMEP
Editorial office: 13–17 Long Lane, London EC1A 9PN

www.rmep.co.uk

RMEP (Religious and Moral Education Press) is an imprint of Hymns Ancient and Modern Ltd (a registered charity), St Mary's Works, St Mary's Plain, Norwich NR3 3BH, UK

Author's acknowledgements

It would not have been possible to write this book without the help, support and patience of many people. Special thanks are due to my family who have patiently put up with rationed time while I have been writing. This book is for my husband James with thanks for all his support, help and abundance of ideas.

Thanks are also due to:
The Jerusalem Trust who provided a bursary under the new writer's scheme.
The Stapleford Centre staff for their support.
Particular thanks go to Alison Farnell for her guidance and to Adrian Brown who was my mentor; the advisory/group who gave feedback on the material – Adrian Brown, Alan Dane, Sue Hookway, Sue Cook, Ann-Marie Brandom, Tom Shaw and Mary Mears; Valerie Bingham for her clarity and attention to detail; my pupils at Preston Manor High School, Wembley, for their honest feedback and enthusiasm.

Text acknowledgements
Bible verses are quoted from the Good News Bible published by The Bible Societies/Harper Collins Publishers Ltd UK © American Bible Society, 1966, 1971, 1976, 1992.
Extracts from *Life of Pi* by Yann Martel, first published in Great Britain by Canongate Books Ltd, 14 High Street, Edinburgh, EH1 1TE.

Photo acknowledgements
Cover and C4: Distorted mirror © Jeff Spirer 2002; A1: Legs © Nikada; A8: Descartes © RMN / Thierry Le Mage, John Locke © Bettmann/CORBIS; B16: John Venn © http://commons.wikimedia. org/wiki/File:John_Venn.jpg, 17/12/2008; C4: Wrong way sign © Krakozawr; C19: Death of Socrates © The Metropolitan Museum of Art, Socrates bust © http://commons.wikimedia. org/wiki/File:Socrates_Pio-Clementino_Inv314.jpg, 15/1/2009; C20: Nelson Mandela © Peter Turnley/CORBIS.

A catalogue record for this book is available from the British Library.

ISBN 978-1-85175-364-2

Illustrated by Clive Wakfer

Designed and Typeset by Topics the Creative Partnership, 397 Topsham Road, Exeter EX2 6HD

Printed and bound in Great Britain by Halstan & Co. Ltd, Amersham, Bucks

Contents

Introduction

Is there a need to teach thinking?

Changes in knowledge, understanding and society are happening so rapidly that it is difficult to know what skills and knowledge will be needed for the future. Teaching thinking will enable our pupils to become reflective, critical and adaptable life-long learners. Teaching thinking skills gives the necessary rigour to the school curriculum that will keep pupils actively engaged and enable them to develop as autonomous, interested learners.

We can categorise types of thinking skills in many ways. One helpful way is to look at the three Cs: critical, caring, and creative thinking. All three types of thinking are skills that are essential for developing 'reasonable' and thoughtful citizens of the future.

Critical thinking – By this we mean thinking associated with good reasoning. We want pupils to become critical thinkers, able to analyse, make inferences and deductions, give reasoned opinions, use precise language, explain what they think clearly, and make reasoned judgements informed by evidence. Pupils also need skills in processing information – to sort, classify, sequence, compare and contrast, evaluate. Thinking tools that support critical thinking in the *Truth-Seekers* series include: Thinker's Hats, PMI (plus, minus or interesting points), connections, mysteries, Diamond 9s, continuum, Venn diagrams and graphic organisers such as concept mapping.

Caring – This refers to thinking that is necessary to become a reasonable person. Essential skills such as active listening, reflecting on one's own behaviour and making sound and fair judgements are prerequisites for good thinking and living in and out of the classroom. Thinking tools that support caring thinking in *Truth-Seekers* include: 'community of enquiry' (see P4C below), guidelines for discussion and accompanying discussion grid.

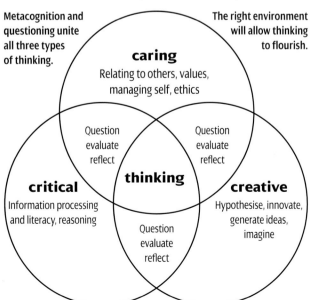

Creative thinking – This type of thinking is often overlooked. However, innovation is the essential component of progress. Critical thinking can help us to analyse the problem, but we need good creative skills to help us move on and further our efforts. We can train ourselves to have a greater flexibility in thinking, to generate new ideas, to be open to future learning and the ideas of others. Thinking tools that support creative thinking in the *Truth-Seekers* series include: 'What if', Thinker's Hats, extended brainstorming, analogies, reverse thinking.

There are many thinking skills strategies that cover one or more of these three types of thinking. Below are a few strategies that can support RE objectives.

Philosophy for Children (P4C)

Philosophy for Children is an international programme for helping pupils to develop skills in critical, caring and creative thinking. The heart of P4C is the 'community of enquiry'. Here pupils work together to generate questions and seek answers in relation to philosophical issues. The teacher's role is to facilitate discussion, steer it gently in the right direction, and to oversee community behaviour.

Method

To be effective, a community of enquiry will generally include the following aspects:

Pupils will sit so that eye contact with every member of the class can be made. This will normally involve pupils sitting in a circle, on the same level with the teacher. Rules will be made by the community and shared. Generally a stimulus will be provided (a text, a picture or an object). There will then be thinking time to reflect on the stimulus. Pupils might be asked to reflect on something puzzling, surprising or interesting. They can record their ideas in individual words or questions. Depending on the resource, teachers might ask pupils what the theme of the story is, or whether they have found something they disagreed with or did not understand. Thinking time is essential at this stage, and it is helpful to have silent individual reflection, before giving an opportunity for paired/group thinking. Ideas are turned into questions which are pooled and written up for all to see. The class (or sometimes the teacher) decides what question is to be answered. Pupils then discuss the issue with guidance from the teacher. Teachers are facilitators of the discussion and help keep the discussion on track, asking probing questions to push for depth. Facilitators will expect reasons and explanations and they should not be afraid of stepping in to draw attention to inconsistencies and irrelevancies, and to extend answers.

Teachers who are unfamiliar with the community of enquiry approach may like to consult a website such as www.sapere.org.uk for greater detail and support.

Creative thinking

Extended brainstorming

Brainstorming is a good activity for fluidity of thought; all ideas are accepted, and piggybacking on others' ideas is allowed. However, during group brainstorming, creative ideas can often be stopped in their tracks by peer comments. To combat this, some class rules for brainstorming can be useful.

Method – the four rules for extended brainstorming

There are four rules for extended brainstorming:

1 Pupils should not make any judgements on ideas.
2 Wacky and exaggerated ideas are to be encouraged.
3 Pupils should go for quantity rather than quality, writing down all suggested ideas.
4 Pupils are allowed to piggyback on other pupils' ideas.

Assessing creative thought is possible, although not clear cut. Teachers may want to assess creative outcomes in the following ways:

- Fluidity/fluency – The number of ideas produced.
- Flexibility – How many different types of idea are generated.
- Originality – Ideas which have not been thought of before (or in the class).
- Elaboration – Which ideas are explained in detail.

Analogies

By using analogies, metaphors and similes, pupils can gain new insights and clarify understanding. When the relationship between two different things is explored, the qualities identified in the more familiar idea help to shed light on the less familiar idea.

Method – looks like, feels like, sounds like

Pupils to create similes to explore a concept, person or thing, for example, Mahatma Gandhi.

Looks like	a frail doily a brewing storm
Feels like	a mosquito bite a strong bear
Sounds like	slippered feet a foghorn

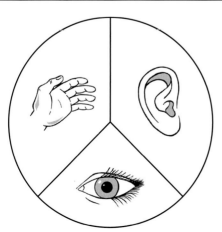

Critical thinking

The six thinking hats (Edward de Bono)

This is a practical method that pupils can use to focus on different aspects of thinking clearly. It can cover critical, caring and creative thinking. Often when discussing issues, pupils' thinking can be clouded by emotions or confusion. By concentrating on different aspects of thinking separately, a clearer picture can be formed. Thinking is divided into six categories, each represented by a different coloured hat. When pupils 'put on' a particular coloured hat, they are thinking in that mode. Thinking hats can be used flexibly: each pupil in a group could use a different hat to answer a key question, or each group in the class could focus on a different hat. Not all hats need be used at once. Looking at difficult ethical issues such as euthanasia, for example, teachers may want pupils to do some red-hat thinking, followed by white-hat thinking. In analysing arguments, the white, yellow and black hats may be used.

Example: The six thinking hats

Type of thinking associated with each hat	Questions that are typically asked
White (Facts)	What information do we currently have? What information do we need?
Red (Feelings)	How do I feel about this? What do I feel about the question?
Yellow (Benefits)	Why will this work? What are the good points about this?
Black (Caution)	What are the problems with this? Will this work?
Green (New ideas)	What is the solution to the problem? What are the alternatives?
Blue (Metacognition)	How well have we worked? What do we need to do next?

Type of thinking associated with each hat	Example question: Does God exist?
White (Facts)	What evidence do we have that God exists?
Red (Feelings)	What are my beliefs about God's existence?
Yellow (Benefits)	What are the strengths of the design argument?
Black (Caution)	What are the limitations and problems with the design argument?
Green (New ideas)	What alternatives are there to the argument for a designer and the cosmological argument to support the existence of God?
Blue (Metacognition)	Can the question of God's existence be answered conclusively? (Explain why or why not?)

What is the aim of the Truth-Seekers series?

The aim of this series is to provide material that introduces the main tenets of philosophy of religion in a rigorous but accessible way. Philosophy of Religion is a rapidly growing area within RE. Many pupils are naturally drawn to philosophical questions. These ultimate questions seek to explore what lies at the heart of human existence, pushing pupils out of their comfort zone, and providing a welcome degree of challenge. Many exam boards are discovering that Philosophy of Religion is becoming one of the most popular options at GCSE and A-Level Religious Studies.

To meet the intellectual demand that philosophical discussion brings, there is an emphasis in the book on developing pupils' thinking skills. There are a variety of thinking tools and strategies used to engage pupils in three different but related types of thinking – critical, caring and creative thinking.

The material does not require pupils to subscribe to any religious or philosophical principle, and at all times pupils are encouraged to think through and analyse their own position. In acknowledging the overall stance of the series, its title, *Truth-Seekers*, reveals its own critical realist approach. This, nevertheless, is not a barrier to pupils (or teachers) personally rejecting the possibility of the existence of truth.

This series would not have been written had it not been for a generous bursary from the Jerusalem Trust for developing Christian-based material. Hence the key questions and activities centre on the western analytical philosophical tradition. There are some suggested references to world religions and other philosophies where appropriate. Many of the activities and thinking tools can be adapted for examination from the perspective of other religions. Ideally, teachers would take the opportunity to explore the key philosophical questions from the perspectives of other world-views. This would support a genuine effort to help pupils seek truth.

How do teachers use this resource?

The three units in this book have been designed so that the material is presented in a logical order, extending and deepening understanding as more concepts are understood. However the material does not have to be followed in the order suggested. Most topics are stand-alone, allowing teachers to dip in and use material that is relevant to their specifications and locally agreed syllabus. The teacher's notes will indicate if the learning in one topic rests upon knowledge of another (see 'prior learning' below).

For teachers looking to use the material to form the basis of a half-term's scheme of work, each unit explores five or six key questions. Core activities are identified in bold in the index of key questions and related activity sheets at the beginning of each unit. In italics are extension activities (covering depth or breadth). Differentiated tasks are provided for each key question.

The book has been designed to incorporate more activities and relevant key questions than could ever be covered in one unit of work. Teachers should feel free to use the material as they wish. Some activities within a topic have the same outcome, but different methods to achieve it, allowing the teacher to choose what is most appropriate for the class. However, a wide range of activities should be tried with the class in order that pupils develop a range of thinking skills. Some differentiated activities will be appropriate for whole class teaching, depending on the age and abilities of the class.

The book is made up of activity sheets and teacher's notes. For most of the activities suggested in the teacher's notes, the worksheets are integral, but there are some that are not worksheet-based. There are many questions prompting further thought on each worksheet. To cater for all pupils, these questions graduate in difficulty. Teachers may like to skip these questions or use them for discussion.

The activity sheets are photocopiable at A5 size or can be enlarged to A4 as preferred. They can also be printed out from the CD-ROM at the back of the book.

What is included in the teacher's notes?

The teacher's notes suggest activities for each of the key questions, together with learning and objectives and outcomes. They also include:

Religious literacy: a list of words to introduce to enable pupils to talk about the topic fluently and with understanding.

Prior learning, which indicates if the learning in one topic rests upon knowledge of another.

Links with cross-curricular topics, other areas within philosophy of religion and links with other units within the *Truth-Seekers* series.

Background: basic information needed for each topic. The teacher's notes provide differentiated activities and ideas for each key question. These can be used to support and extend pupils throughout KS3 and KS4. In each unit there are some additional differentiated worksheets and writing frames.

There is an assessment example at the beginning of each unit, with suggested levels and outcomes.

Unit A **The theory of knowledge**

About the unit

This unit suggests activities and support material to examine what we can know. Many religious groups claim to have knowledge about God. Some of these claims to knowledge are grounded in experience, some reason and some a mixture of the two. Different claims to knowledge about God between and within religions can appear contradictory. In this context the questions of what is knowledge and how we gain knowledge are important.

This topic introduces pupils to the basic elements of epistemology (the theory of knowledge). Pupils will look at the place of reason and experience in producing knowledge, and the pitfalls of relying on either. Pupils will also consider how belief differs from knowledge and the relationships between belief, truth and certainty. They will look at the role of scepticism and its relationship with religious claims to knowledge.

This unit does not need to be taught prior to other units of work in Philosophy of Religion. However, it does enhance understanding in topics such as Experiencing God and the Existence of God.

Where this unit fits in

This unit links with the following Key Stage 3 guidelines in the non-statutory national framework for RE:

- Learning about religion: 1d, 1e, 1f, 1g
- Learning from religion: 2a, 2e
- Religions and beliefs: 3a, 3d (adaptable for 3b)
- Themes: is applicable from 3e to 3l
- Experiences and opportunities: 3o, 3p

This unit serves as a base for the other units, in particular for arguments about the existence of God, or looking at the nature of God.

The sceptic's challenge is covered in several GCSE specifications and the extent of our knowledge. Identifying different types of knowledge is on the AQA GCSE specification B. The Theory of Knowledge is a set module for the International Baccalaureate.

Attitudes in the unit

This unit helps pupils develop the following four attitudes outlined in the non-statutory national framework for RE:

Self awareness Developing a realistic and positive sense of their own religious, moral and spiritual ideas, *e.g. in coming to understand why they hold their beliefs.*

Respect for all Developing skills of listening and a willingness to learn from others, even when others' views are different from their own, *e.g. when exploring different attitudes and conceptions of knowledge.*

Open-mindedness Distinguishing between opinions, viewpoints and beliefs in connection with issues of conviction and faith, *e.g. in examining how knowledge is different from belief.*

Appreciation and wonder Developing their imagination and curiosity, *e.g. by asking questions about puzzling aspects of life and moral and religious issues through ignorance logging.*

Learning objectives and outcomes

Pupils will consider the difference between fact, opinion and belief and analyse their own religious knowledge into these three categories. They will look at to what extent we can rely on experience for our foundations of knowledge, and the impact this has for religious claims about God that are grounded in experience. They will also look at the role of reason in religious knowledge, and consider the limits of reason as a useful way of discovering knowledge about God.

At lower levels: pupils will understand that there are different types of knowledge and this can be gained through experience or reasoning. They will understand that opinion is different from knowledge (knowledge is inseparable from certainty) and that will limit what we can know about God.

At higher levels: pupils might look at Locke's theory of primary and secondary qualities and the Gettier examples. They will consider the sceptic's challenge and formulate a response to Descartes.

Assessment example

(based on activity in the Teacher's Notes p. 19) **'Is it possible to know God? If so, how do believers gain knowledge of God?'**

Prior knowledge – pupils need to have covered the strengths and weaknesses of both the rationalist and empiricist models for knowledge. Before this assessment teachers should discuss with pupils how knowledge about God is different from knowledge about things in the material world. Pupils should have a basic understanding of God's nature (*Truth-Seekers: Thinking about the Nature of God*, Unit A). Pupils who have studied arguments for God's existence and religious experience (*Truth-Seekers: Thinking about God*, Units A and B) are likely show greater understanding in their answers. This is a challenging question and is more suited to older KS3 and KS4 pupils.

Level 4: Pupils working at level 4 will be able to describe some of the different ways in which we gain knowledge. They will refer to both experience and reasoning and will be able to explain at least one weakness of each as a method of gaining knowledge of God. They will show some understanding of some of the ways that people experience God. This may include prayer, revelation, miracles and religious experiences. They will reach a personal conclusion to the question.

Level 5: Pupils working at level 5 may explain that God is transcendent (although they may not necessarily use technical vocabulary). They will refer to both rationalism and empiricism in their answer, linking this with knowledge about God. They will be able to describe some of the limitations of empiricism and rationalism in gaining knowledge about God. They will show some understanding of some of the ways that people experience God. This may include prayer, revelation, miracles and religious experiences.

Level 6: Pupils working at level 6 will be able to use philosophical and religious vocabulary to give an informed answer to the question. They will give a fair account of the limitations of rationalism and empiricism. They will link this with knowledge about God, providing specific examples of religious claims to knowledge that are either rationalist or empiricist. They may refer to the difference between fact, belief and opinion, explaining the grounds for religious belief, but how this differs from certainty.

Level 7: Pupils working at level 7 will be able to use a strong philosophical and religious vocabulary to give a coherent understanding of the issues. They will be able to describe, illustrate and evaluate the different ways in which we gain knowledge. These they will relate to knowledge about God. They will briefly refer to the nature of God, explaining how the transcendence of God will affect our understanding. They will be able to refer to specific examples of religious experience and analyse these in the context of the question. They may (if it has been referred to in class) make reference to Kierkegaard's rejection of objective knowledge about God and the need to make a leap of faith.

Useful background resources

Teacher books: *Meditations on First Philosophy* – René Descartes

Films: *The Matrix* I and II; *The Truman Show*
TV: 'Who shot Mr Burns?' – *The Simpsons*

Religious literacy

Through the activities in this unit pupils will understand, use and spell correctly the following words and terms: *belief, empiricism, evidence, experience, fact, grounds for reasons, inductive, justified, knowledge, opinion, rationalism.*

Index of key questions and related activity sheets

Note: **core activities are listed in bold**; *extension activities are listed in italic.*

Teacher's notes: 1. What is the difference between fact, opinion and belief?

Suggested teaching activities

A1 Fact, opinion, belief

- Ask pupils to write down an example of a fact, then an opinion and then a belief. These could be done alone or written up on the board. Pupils could have collected examples in advance through a homework questionnaire. These should be shared.

- Alternatively the teacher could ask several pupils to share understanding in one area – e.g. the Sikh gurus. These could be collected on the board and then analysed in groups, placing them into a table of facts, opinions and beliefs. On the basis of this, teachers could ask pupils to define fact, opinion and belief. This could be done in pairs, cascading, to revise the definitions. Alternatively this could be done as part of a community of enquiry.

- Pupils could use sheet **A1**, analysing the passages. (Leave the religious knowledge section until later in the lesson.) Pupils should be able to define fact, opinion and belief accurately.

- Ask for a volunteer/s to come to the front of the classroom and talk for one minute on any subject (the teacher can set the topic: religious, or controversial, or one that will generate bias, such as football teams). The other pupils should record his/her statements and whether they are facts, opinions or beliefs. This is more effective if the volunteers do not know that the others will be judging their statements on those criteria.

- Pupils could think of a set of 10 statements concerning religion. These should be sorted into facts, opinions and beliefs.

- The following questions could be discussed:
  - Are religious statements more likely to be facts, beliefs or opinions? Give reasons why.
  - What sort of religious statements tend to be facts?
  - Can we ever have true religious knowledge?
  - What conditions would there need to be to turn religious beliefs into religious knowledge?

- Teachers could focus on this last distinction, using the supplementary sheet **A2** *Separating fact from opinion*. This sheet contains words that are often associated with the definition of fact, opinion and belief.

Pupils should cut out/be given the cards on the sheet, and divide them up into words that are closest to the meaning of fact, opinion and belief. Pupils should justify why they have placed particular words in a particular category. This is especially important in the case of words that they find difficult to place, or are ambiguous.

Pupils could then use the triangle to help them rank the words: which are closest in meaning to fact, opinion and belief? This should help them to define the words more accurately, and assess at which stage the associated meanings blur.

Then pupils should place each word appropriately somewhere along one side of the triangle, depending on whether it is nearer a fact/opinion, belief/fact or opinion/belief. The words closest to fact, opinion or belief should be placed near the appropriate corner.

Learning objectives and outcomes

To differentiate between a fact, an opinion and a belief.

Synopsis

A1: Can you distinguish what is factually true?

A Neasden United supporter praises her team – but how much of what she is saying is fact?

Religious literacy: Words to be introduced – fact, opinion, belief, knowledge, evidence. (Definitions of these words can be found in the summary sheet, **A14**.)

Prior learning: None necessary.

Links: The information in this topic is essential as a preface to the rest of this unit on the theory of knowledge. Identifying facts, beliefs and opinions also ties in with concerns of truth (How do we reach truth? Is there a truth?) and proof (What do we need to do with belief for it to become knowledge?) These links can be found in *Truth-Seekers: Thinking about God.* There are also links with scientific enquiry: in particular, whether we can be certain of anything at all.

Teachers may like to use this topic as a starting point to examining religious knowledge, in particular religious traditions. In most cases, this arises from revelation and religious experience. Pupils could examine revelation in a particular tradition, and assess whether this is truly knowledge or not. Pupils might also look at religious creeds.

For **Background**, see p. 11.

Pupils working at higher levels

- Take a daily newspaper and study an article of your choice. (Broadsheets and tabloids are equally useful, depending on the pupils' age and ability.)
  - Highlight facts, opinions and beliefs in different colours.
  - Work out the factual percentage of the story.
  - Is the journalist trying to pass off a belief or an opinion as a fact? What wording tells you that this is the case?

- Pupils to think of examples where there is some ambiguity concerning opinions and beliefs. Why is there difficulty in deciding between the two?

- Make up a test to differentiate between fact, opinion and belief. This might be a set of questions that people could ask of each statement. Pupils could try this out on statements that people have collected.

- A few pupils could focus on what the RE teacher says in a 20-minute period. What proportion of teacher talk is fact, opinion or belief? What other category of statements did they use?

- What sort of evidence is necessary to turn an opinion or belief into a fact? Pupils could think about whether we have solid evidence for anything. They could ask their science teachers to give examples of scientific 'facts' that now have been falsified, or do some research themselves.

Pupils working at lower levels

To reinforce the idea before the worksheet is started, pupils may need more practice with differentiating fact, opinion and belief – especially the latter two. The teacher could give pupils some marked and simple statements, e.g.
  - I like sweets.
  - March comes before April.
  - It might rain on Tuesday.
  - There is a heaven.

- Pupils could make a fact, opinion and belief game. They could compile 30 or more statements, each written on a piece of card the size of a playing card. The game should be played a bit like snap. The cards should be upside down. Pupils should each decide whether they are looking for a fact, opinion or a belief. Each player turns one card over. If the statement matches the type of statement they are looking for they should shout it out and place their hand on the card. The person with the most cards wins.

- Pupils working at lower levels may struggle with the last activity on the sheet. If they do then the following questions (to be asked of each statement) may help them:
  - Think of whether anyone would disagree with the statement. What might they say? If no one disagrees with the statement then it is more likely to be factual.
  - What evidence have you that the statement is correct?
  - Is the evidence strong or weak?
  - Would you trust the evidence? Why or why not?

Teacher's notes: 2. What is knowledge?

Suggested teaching activities

To enable pupils to get the most out of this topic, it is important to preface the relevant worksheet (**A5**) with thinking about knowledge in general:

- Pupils have three minutes to jot down 20 examples of things that they know. They should share this with a partner or group. Pupils to try and categorise their examples if possible into different kinds (e.g. facts, mathematical, scientific, aesthetic, religious, etc.) using colours or highlighters. Pupils to share with the class any examples that were hard to place or ambiguous.

- Pupils could use the supplementary sheet *A3 Quotes on knowledge* to spark off a debate about the nature of knowledge. These quotes can be differentiated if required. Those quotes surrounded by dotted lines are the easiest to understand, and hence will be more accessible for pupils working at lower levels. Those in dashed lines are aimed at those who are more able. Pupils should be given an opportunity to provide quotes of their own on knowledge. The class could also examine quotes from contemporary musicians and actors.

Among many other things, pupils could:

– Pick out the three quotes that sum up what knowledge is, explaining their reasons. Pupils could then discuss why they have chosen these, with a partner. They could aim to persuade their partner that their quotes best represent knowledge (and vice versa).

– Cut up the quotes and sort them into two piles, ones they agree with and ones they disagree with. Then in the 'agree' pile, they could rank the cards (linear or in a diamond shape) with ones they agree with most at the top.

– Pupils could take the King quote and the Whitehead quote, which both centre around the word 'ignorance' and discuss whether they contradict each other or not. Why or why not? (They do not.)

– Pupils could evaluate particular quotes (see Unit B). They could return to this sheet at the end of this unit and see whether they have changed their mind.

- Below are some questions and activities based on the individual quotes. These might be used orally, or as an extension task.

Confucius – Pupils to reflect on whether they ever thought that they knew something only to discover that they did not know it so well. What might this tell us about the nature of knowledge?

Thomas Sowell – How do we turn ideas into knowledge? Have you any ideas or theories? How would we prove them true? Try to find a religious idea. What would we need to prove it true? Find out about knowledge that was once believed, but now rebuked, e.g. Copernican revolution, and debunking the existence of phlogiston.

A. N. Whitehead – Is this true? Why is it true? Highlight anything you need more information on in an ignorance log. What are your known unknowns about X religion?

Martin Luther King – Find an example to illustrate King's quote. Religious intolerance and examples of racism may be used.

Arthur Schopenhauer – Read a news article/religious belief. Rewrite the article from the opposite perspective (e.g. Jesus' miracles from the point of view of a first-century Jew). Write some guidelines for extending our horizons.

Learning objectives and outcomes

To consider the nature of knowledge.

To reflect on what things pupils are certain about.

Synopsis

A3: A collection of quotes on knowledge provides stimulus in thinking about knowledge.

Background: The contrast between facts, beliefs and opinion can help us better understand what knowledge is. In all three we are asserting that something is the case. With belief and opinion it is likely that others will hold views contrary to us. With knowledge this can also be the case, although that person would be wrong to do so. This begs the question, how are we to secure knowledge from mere opinion? Sufficient evidence will be required. In turn we must ask, what is sufficient evidence? Do we ever have enough evidence to cite something as fact or knowledge? Similarly, it is important to distinguish a correct but unfounded opinion from one which is backed up with strong evidence. The former, according to Plato, would not be knowledge. The latter some may claim could be deemed knowledge, but there are still difficulties with maintaining this. See Background for **A5** on p.13.

Pupils working at higher levels

- Pupils could try to define and give examples of scientific, musical, factual, aesthetic, moral and religious knowledge (there are many more types that could be included), giving examples of each.
  Then they could try to explain the difference between these. Do they have a common thread running through?

- Pupils could invent their own sayings about knowledge. These could be evaluated and displayed.

- Pupils could examine religious knowledge. In past times RE was called RK in some countries. Was this RE or rather Religious Instruction? What might RK amount to in reality, and is it possible to have religious knowledge?

- 'Pupils could try to explain what knowledge is through a Socratic dialogue exercise.

- Pupils to work out a working definition for knowledge. When they have come up with a definition, peers should assess it to see if they can find any flaws.

- Pupils to discuss whether knowledge is justified true belief. Can pupils think of examples where someone who has justified true belief still cannot be said to have knowledge? Pupils could look at Edmund Gettier's famous examples that dispute that knowledge is justified true belief. (http://www3.sympatico.ca/saburns/pg0306b.htm).

Pupils working at lower levels

- Pupils to make a knowledge log. They should spend five minutes writing down examples of things that they know. They could then do some of the following:

- Split their list into the following three categories:
  – Knowing things
  – Knowing how to . . .
  – To know (recognise)
  (Some pupils might like to make a Venn diagram to show the overlap between these areas.)

- Split their list into things they know really well, know quite well and not well at all.

- Pupils to look at different types of knowledge. Pupils to be given a list of professions (e.g. doctor, artist, farmer, writer, teacher, cleaner). What knowledge does each of them need to carry out their job properly (e.g. doctor needs factual medical knowledge, perhaps of surgery, biology, good reading and writing skills, clear communication skills, a good ethical sense, understanding of people, etc). This could be expanded to discover how the person gain their knowledge.

- 'He who is wise knows he knows not' – Socrates). Pupils could examine this quote and the extent to which it is true. It might be interesting to tell pupils that the amount of knowledge a Year 12 is exposed to in that one year is the same amount of knowledge that their grandparents would have been exposed to in a lifetime; or that by the time a child born this year gets to Year 3, the amount of knowledge in the world will have quadrupled.

Teacher's notes: 2. What is knowledge?

Will Durant – How does the parable of the three tenants relate to Durant's quote? Do we have a responsibility to use our talents? What talents do you have? How might you use them to greater effect (set a goal)? Find out about liberation theology. Does this branch of theology exemplify Christian ideals? Look at a problem such as world poverty. Who is more at fault? The person who ignores an issue, despite condemning it academically, or a person who is ignorant of the issue and does not think about it? Why? How might you put one of your beliefs into action?

Leonardo da Vinci – What does he mean? Would Christian Evangelists agree or disagree?

Albert Einstein (amount of knowledge) – Research the rate of knowledge increase in the world. What things would you most like to find out? What questions would you ask God if you could? If you could only pass on three important pieces of information to your children, what would they be and why? (This task could be connected with a unit on holy books such as the Torah.) What are the three important pieces of knowledge for Sikhs/Hindus/Muslims/etc.?

Seneca – Predict what things will be discovered/invented in the next century (predictions could be given under the categories of home, school and religion).

Francis Bacon – What makes us human? In what way is Bacon correct? Are you more than the sum of your knowledge? Explain in what way.

Goethe – Draw a diagram to illustrate Goethe's quote. In the centre of a page write down a piece of (religious) knowledge. Around it place questions which arise from it to show how our doubt has grown.

Oscar Wilde – How might a teacher react to this quote? Do you agree? Are we solely taught about God, or is it innate? What is your greatest learning experience (inside or outside of school)?

Albert Einstein (grandmother) – Why does Einstein choose a grandmother here? What is the most difficult thing that you have learned in RE this year? Explain it in simple terms for a young child or for a grandparent.

Aristotle – Is this always true? Is this true in the case of religions and miracles?

Cullen Hightower – Think of an example to illustrate this quote. How might some religious people agree with Hightower? Do we 'refuse' to get the message? Which messages should we accept? Find out about a religious person who 'refused' to get the message initially (e.g. Doubting Thomas). What made them accept the message? How do we know if a message has been given? (Links can be made with this quote and Buddhism and enlightenment.)

Socrates – Solve this paradox: Can you have complete knowledge of everything? How do you know when you have reached complete knowledge?

- Pupils could try to form an initial definition of knowledge. (This could be done now or later as a community of enquiry.)

- Pupils could assess the belief that 'God exists'. What conditions would have to be met to make their belief into knowledge? Students could discuss what conditions have already been met, and which ones have not yet been met.

Pupils working at higher levels

- Older (Year 11+), more able pupils can have a go at modifying JTB (justified true belief) to improve the definition of knowledge.

- Pupils to discuss – What problems can you see with defining knowledge as something that cannot be mistaken?

Pupils working at lower levels

- Pupils could make an ignorance log. This log could be used for any project across subject areas and asks pupils to identify a lack of knowledge in a particular area. (In RE in particular it could be used to great effect in generating ultimate questions, and provide some support in working out what knowledge is necessary in seeking the answer.)

Pupils could use the sheet **A4 Ignorance log**, to help them. Pupils brainstorm areas where they lack knowledge. From that they can formulate one question to which they would like the answer. Then pupils need to generate as many questions as they can which will help them understand the initial question.

Teacher's notes: 2. What is knowledge?

Suggested teaching activities

A5 What is knowledge?

- Read the sheet A5 as a class. Below are some supporting examples:

True belief

Zara is two years old. Her mummy told her that on Tuesday she would go to the playground. Zara woke up on both Sunday and Monday and announced that it was Tuesday. She woke up the next day and was correct when she said it was Tuesday. They had a lovely time at the playground. Zara's belief that today was the day she would go to the playground was true, but can we say she had knowledge of this?

Imagine the following scenario: A Christian believed in God all her life because her parents brought her up to believe in Christianity. She died and went to heaven with God. Would you say that she knew during her lifetime that God existed?

Justified belief

I belief that Sid Shady stole the money from the bank. He has committed many bank robberies before. He was seen at the bank at the time of the crime, jumping into his Mercedes with a handful of money. His fingerprints were also on the door of the bank. However, in reality Sid only went to the bank to take out some cash from the cashpoint. He leant against the door of the bank to see if it was open. Having got his money he ran back to his car as it was starting to rain. In fact, the real criminal was a little old lady who was there at the same time as Sid.

Imagine the following scenario: A Christian believed in God because the Bible had told her to and because she had had a religious experience. Would you say that she had knowledge of God's existence?

- Pupils to write down 10 things that they believe. How many of these things can they know for certain? For each belief, they should say whether it is true, and explain their justification for believing it.

- Pupils to read the Zarg Report on sheet *A6 How knowledgeable are the Zarg?* This is an exercise on identifying justified beliefs, true beliefs, and justified true beliefs. Pupils should identify any knowledge and also statements that are not true pieces of knowledge. Pupils to consider to what extent the Zarg are correct. They should give the reason why in each case. A summary of the answers is as follows:

Justified belief	True belief	Justified true belief
People visit hot countries in the winter.	People wear football shirts.	Need air to survive.
Black box in the corner of the room.	Honey comes from bees.	
People like work.		

Learning objectives and outcomes

To explore definitions of knowledge.

To reflect on the boundaries between belief and certainty.

To identify true beliefs, justified beliefs, opinion and knowledge.

Synopsis

A5: We claim to have knowledge of many things. However, what do we really mean when we say we know something?

A6: This story explores how much we really know.

The Zarg, aliens from the planet Zog, have submitted a report to the officials on Zarg based on their knowledge of earth so far. How much knowledge have they really amassed?

Religious literacy: Words to be introduced – justified true belief (JTB).

Prior learning: None necessary.

Links: Philosophy (epistemology); International Baccalaureate's Theory of Knowledge specification.

Pupils working at higher levels

- Pupils to take each of the Zarg's points and write them as formal arguments. Pupils could then assess their validity. (See Unit B: Arguing effectively for information on making arguments.) An example is below:

  Premise 1 Birds migrate to warm places.
  Premise 2 Some humans migrate to warm places.
  Conclusion Humans are birds.
  (This is an invalid argument.)

- Research some religious miracles, e.g. Ganesh drinking milk in Neasden and Ealing (London), Allah's name appearing in a fish. What conclusions might someone jump to on the basis of the available evidence? What other evidence would you look to in verifying these miracles? What would be strong grounds for believing these miracles. (For information about grounds of reasons, see Unit B Arguing effectively.)

Pupils working at lower levels

- Pupils to think about a time where they have jumped to conclusions based on one piece of evidence.

- Pupils could write a story about how easy (and misleading) it can be to jump to conclusions.

- Some students may find it easier to analyse the Zarg Report in a table format (see below).

	Evidence given	Evidence needed
Birds		
Football		
Honey		
Work		
Pets		
Air		

Background: At the heart of epistemology is the question of what is knowledge. This has been traditionally defined as justified true belief. However, Edmund Gettier sparked off rigorous debate when he provided counter-examples to this formula. He cited examples where a belief was true and the person justified in believing it. However, the fact that it was true only related to the justification through chance.

Many responses to Gettier have centred around additional clauses to JTB that will satisfy knowledge. However, the extent that these have been successful is debatable. Some commentators believe that these are doomed to the same problems that Gettier highlighted. If this is the case then it appears that knowledge cannot be defined adequately.

Teacher's notes: 3. How do we gain knowledge?

Suggested teaching activities

A7 *How well do you know your stuff?*

- Pupils have a 0–10 scale. The teacher reads out a list of statements (or uses the ones on the sheet). Pupils rank each one on how well they think they know them.
Pupils should write next to each mark how they have come to gain knowledge about the thing, e.g. they will have knowledge of spaghetti bolognese from eating it, or eating several versions, or looking at a picture in a cook book, or hearing someone talk about it.

A lot of discussion can be generated about how well we can know things. For example, if the subject is Las Vegas, they might know it from an episode of *The Simpsons*, or from a book/world map or watching the news. Maybe Granny visited the USA and brought back a cheesy T-shirt. Maybe they have been/lived there. Maybe they just have preconceptions of Americans.

Other things that could be ranked well are places and people (including pop and film stars, friends, family, themselves), giving reasons how they have gained the knowledge and also reasons why they do not know them completely.

- This could be expanded. Pupils could look at the completed scale and work out in pairs the different ways we learn that something exists.
- Pupils could brainstorm how many different ways we can know something. They should be able to get at least the main three: direct experience, working things out through reasoning, and testimony. This can be extended by considering whether our knowledge about God is in a different category to other forms of knowledge.

Learning objectives and outcomes

To examine knowledge and consider the grounds for holding knowledge.

To explore how deeply that knowledge is held.

To identify the different ways we gain knowledge.

Synopsis

A7: How do we learn that something exists?

We learn either through inference or deduction from something other than itself, or through direct experience (or the direct experience of others).

How reliant are we on experience for our knowledge?

Religious literacy: Words to be introduced – experience, direct experience, testimony, reliability, testing. Words to be introduced at a higher level – inference, deduction, induction.

Prior learning: None necessary.

Links: There are links here with religious experience and how we can know God. Specifically there are links with sheet **B1 Knowing God** in *Truth-Seekers: Thinking about God*. There are also links with Unit B **Arguing effectively**; in particular, thinking and assessing grounds for reasons.

Pupils working at higher levels

- Pupils could aim to rank on the 0–10 scale pieces of abstract knowledge given by the teacher. They could extend this work by giving details of what they would need to do in order to develop their knowledge. (The sheet **A4 Ignorance log** would be a good scaffold for this.)

- Once pupils have categorised the different ways of getting to know something, they can decide which they think is the most reliable. They should explain their answers.

- Pupils could consider whether we need absolute knowledge of the world, or whether this is unnecessary and/or impossible. Can we say that we have true knowledge of anything, and if so, what?

- Pupils can examine the limitations of their knowledge of a subject through a community of enquiry, or through the sheet **B19 Defining moments** in Unit B.

- Pupils could research how other species perceive the world, e.g. bats and dolphins use of sonar. What implications does this have for our ability to know the world.

Pupils working at lower levels

If pupils are stuck then the teacher could ask some direct questions to prompt them, such as:

– Have you experienced it?
– Describe your experience of it.

This might be done as a planning map or chart.

- In groups, pupils could be given an artefact. Pupils could make a list of everything they know about the artefact from observation.

Do pupils consider that they 'know' that artefact now? What don't they know about the artefact? In what ways have they not experienced the artefact?

Background: We do not know things as well as we might think we do. This will become apparent to pupils if they try having a Socratic style dialogue on any topic (see sheet **B19 Defining moments**). Some philosophers go as far as to say that we do not have full knowledge of anything. Our ways of discovering new knowledge is limited to that learned through our five senses and reasoning. We only have to look at bats, whales and dogs to see that they approach the world through different means, and hence will gain different knowledge of the world as a result. We have to ask in response, what can be practically and satisfactorily accepted as proper knowledge?

Teacher's notes: 3. How do we gain knowledge?

Suggested teaching activities

A8 How do we gain our knowledge?

- Pupils to individually brainstorm as many facts as they can about the world in three minutes. They should share these with a group. Pupils to work out how they got each piece of knowledge. Pupils should then look at their lists and try to categorise the types of knowledge.

- In pairs, pupils should write down the things that a child will learn in the first year of life. They will notice that all knowledge will be related to experiences. When (if at all) does this change?

- Pupils to brainstorm in groups what they have learned through reasoning this week. They should then underline any reasoning that had significant input from their senses. Was there any knowledge gained solely through reasoning with no reference to experience?

- Pupils to do questions (a)–(g), working out which statements are known through rationalism and which are empirically based.

  Answers:
  Rationally based – (a), (e), (d), (g)
  Empirically based – (b), (f)
  Rational or empirical – (c) (this could be discovered by working out the link rationally, or through experience)

- Pupils to discuss whether knowledge about God and claims to religious truth are rationally or empirically based. Pupils to give examples.

Learning objectives and outcomes

To use rational and empirically-based categories for knowledge.

Synopsis

A8: Looks at different types of knowledge

Pupils look at how they gain their knowledge. Is it experience based, reason-based, or a combination of both?

Religious literacy: Words to be introduced – empirical, reason, rationalism, knowledge.

Prior learning: None necessary.

Links: Science.

Pupils working at higher levels

- Pupils could research/discuss the nature/existence of innate knowledge. (Ask students to think of animal behaviour or the sucking action of newborn babies. Can this be called real knowledge?) Locke dismissed any idea of innate knowledge.

- Pupils could also discuss the place of genes in our ability to reason, and whether genetic factors are as important as our experience in determining what knowledge we will gain.

- Pupils to consider whether claims to knowledge are stronger if they are empirically or rationally based.

Pupils working at lower levels

- In groups, pupils could do a short role-play to explain how young children gain knowledge. One child can vocalise the child's thought processes while the others act. This could be done as an improvisation with a confident group.

  Other groups can do the same, but with the focus on a 7-year-old child, an 11-year-old and a 16-year-old.

  A follow-up discussion could focus on when reasoning comes into play, and whether reasoning is derived from experience or not.

- Pupils to work out whether scientific and mathematical knowledge are gained through empiricism or rationalism. Pupils can look up examples of famous mathematicians and scientists who have discovered new knowledge and see if their own conclusions are correct.

Background: Rationalism is the view that we cannot gain true understanding or knowledge of the world through experience. This is because our senses can give inaccurate information, are often subjective and the information we receive can be coloured by emotion and motivation, etc. Moreover, physical objects in the world are impermanent.

Only reason can give us true knowledge of what things are. Empiricism is the view that all our knowledge about the world is gained through experience. This can include experimenting through our senses and reflection from this.

Teacher's notes: 4. Can we rely on experience?

Suggested teaching activities

A9 Can our senses deceive us?

- Pupils need to be provided with the materials for these tests. They are easily obtained and are useful examples, but there is much flexibility in using whatever is at hand. The aim of the experiments is to see how accurate their senses are. The worksheet has a suggested list of materials and experiments.

- Pupils can be provided with a set of optical illusions to illustrate how our sense of perception can be deceptive. A range of optical illusions can be found at the following websites:

  http://listverse.com/miscellaneous/20-amazing-optical-illusions
  www.eyetricks.com/illusions.htm
  www.at-bristol.org.uk/optical/default.htm
  www.echalk.co.uk/amusements/OpticalIllusions/illusions.aspx

  A popular illusion is the Necker cube. This cube can be visually interpreted in two different ways, often appearing to flip back and forth. Another useful illusion to use in class is the Zollner illusion. The thick lines are parallel, but the opposing lines make them look as if they are not.

  An online senses challenge can be found at: www.bbc.co.uk/science/humanbody/body/interactives/senseschallenge.

- Pupils can discuss the question: 'If our senses can deceive us, then can we be sure of anything?' There is a thinking and talking grid to aid with this question (A12) and this should be used in conjunction with the guidelines for group discussion (A13). This is linked to A11 **The Great Deception**, and teacher's notes can be found on p. 19.

- Pupils to discuss: What knowledge do we gain from perception of the world around us? (colours, sounds, smells, tastes, heat or cold, the shape of the environment around us).

- Some pupils might like to discuss how clothing styles and colours can affect the way we are perceived.

- Pupils to devise a test to show how our perception of something can alter due to an emotional response, or because of a set context or situation.

Learning objectives and outcomes

To experience how sense can deceive.

To evaluate whether we can be certain of anything.

Synopsis

A9: Are our senses always reliable? Pupils put four of their senses to the test with these practical experiments.

A10: Pupils look at optical illusions to assess the liability of their sense of sight.

Religious literacy: Words to be introduced – perception.

Prior learning: None necessary.

Links: Psychology, biology, sociology.

Background: Our senses can often be unreliable and can give us false knowledge. This has led some people to assert that we cannot truly know things empirically. Most people have mistaken things, based on sound or sight. This is especially true if we have to rely on less of a sense than we are used to (such as our colour vision at night time, or our sense of smell when we have a cold). Optical illusions make the point very clearly. In an optical illusion, there are at least two ways to look at one thing. In the absence of clear information, our brain makes a choice for us, even though we might not realise this. Through perception, we gain knowledge of the world around us. However, this information does not come to us directly; it is processed through information channels, coded physiologically, and then interpreted by the brain. This is not to say, however, that our experiences of the world are indirect. Perception of the world around us can be altered through the context in which we are experiencing a thing, or by our emotion or motivation. For example, the perception of smell consists not only of the sensation of the odours themselves but of the experiences and emotions associated with these sensations. Smells can evoke strong emotional reactions and can alter how we perceive the smell, or the thing associated with the smell (and vice versa). Even our perception of flavour can be altered by the colour or texture of food.

Pupils working at higher levels

- Pupils could analyse the testing methods on sheet A9 to ensure that they are fair. Could they improve on the methodology?

- Alternatively, pupils could work without the sheet. They could be given a challenge to make a fair experiment that will test the accuracy of senses. The key thing here is to ensure that no other sense can interfere with the testing of one sense. Information about fair tests can be found at: http://www.ise5-14.org.uk/Prim3/New_Guidelines/Investigations/Menu.htm

- Pupils can research or invent their own optical illusions.

- Pupils could debate if there are more than five senses.

- Pupils to analyse in depth which elements of sensory data prove the most problematic. They should devise scientific hypotheses and carry out experiments to this end. Is this the same for everybody? Pupils could then examine religious experience accounts and see if any of the 'weak spots' for the senses overlap with the accounts. Do the conclusions help us in any way in assessing the validity of experience claims?

- Pupils to see if they can devise a fair test for assessing the validity of a religious experience. They can try the test out using fake claims and genuine claims. If the tests do not work, students must be able to explain why this is so, and how they would adapt them.

Pupils working at lower levels

- Pupils could list the five senses. For each they should make a list of everyday things we cannot do/would find difficult without that sense.

- Pupils (in groups) could decide an order of importance for the five senses. This could be run according to different criteria, e.g. senses that:
  – are the most reliable.
  – give us the most information about the world.
  – enable us to function in the world most effectively.

  Alternatively, in groups of five each member could be a spokesperson for one 'sense', arguing why their sense is the most essential and most reliable.

- Pupils could role-play a situation where emotion affects perception. Alternatively, pupils could write a short story on 'wrong perception', based on how their initial perceptions about something/someone were affected by emotional aspects.

Teacher's notes: 5. Can we rely on reason?

Suggested teaching activities

A10 *It's all a matter of evidence*

- Each group should get a pack of cards. The evidence cards should be printed on a different colour to the scenario cards. The cards should be pre-cut and placed in an envelope. There is an empty template for scenarios and evidence that students or teachers could use.
  1 Each group of four must at random take one scenario card and then three evidence cards.
  2 Students then need to work out what must have happened to cause the scenario using only the evidence available. (The evidence must be integral to the solution). Additional characters may be added to the story.
  3 One person should be the leader, responsible for ensuring that everyone has given an opinion, and for governing the selection process for the solution.
  4 They should then record their answers on the template sheet (A10 continued: It's all a matter of solutions).

- Please note that there are no formal answers to this creative thinking game. Students must think imaginatively, and sometimes laterally, to gain a solution. This game could also be played as a whole-class activity.

- A version of this game could be played in fours with no cards. One pupil writes a scenario on a piece of paper and folds it over. She passes this to number 2 who writes a piece of evidence and folds it over. He passes this to 3 and then 4 who do the same as 2. Then they all unravel the paper and find a solution to the scenario using clues.

- After this game, it is beneficial to hear completed examples from the class. Pupils can discuss the evidence provided and explore what evidence might be needed in order to make the evidence more conclusive in each case. To what extent can we draw conclusions from limited evidence?

- After the game, pupils are given the conclusion 'God exists'. Pupils each to take on the role of a religious believer (from a different denomination or religion). Pupils to think of simple evidence that could be used from the natural world to enable the conclusion to be reached. Or they could think of evidence on a broad scale and include experience or revelation that is within the context of a/many religion/s. Pupils to consider whether the evidence provided is a one-off occurrence, or whether there are lots of examples of this type of evidence or observation. They can then discuss whether the amount of evidence provided is strong enough to form a generalised conclusion that God exists. (See induction notes in Background.)

- *The Simpsons* episode 'Who Shot Mr Burns?' can be a useful way to explore the use of evidence. Pupils could be asked to examine the case based on the evidence (withholding the ending where Homer is in hospital) and then based on what really happened.

- Some pupils could extend their understanding by looking at the difference between inductive and deductive reasoning. If pupils will also be covering syllogisms from the unit: Arguing Effectively, a clear distinction will be easy to make (these are all deductive arguments). See Background for a fuller explanation on the difference. Pupils might begin by thinking about how they learn from experience and provide examples. This is inductive reasoning in everyday life.

Learning objectives and outcomes

To consider how evidence is used to reach conclusions.

To use creative thinking to reach explanations.

Synopsis

A10: A game of induction.

To play a game of evidence. Students are invited to use their creative intelligence to infer (or surmise) what has happened in each scenario with randomly picked pieces of evidence.

Religious literacy: Words to be introduced – evidence and possibly induction and deduction.

Prior learning: None necessary.

Links: Scientific enquiry, English.

Background: Inductive reasoning is used to formulate generalisations or laws based on a number of observations or experiences of the same kind of thing. For instance, if we have only ever seen white swans, it would be reasonable to conclude that all swans are white. Each additional observation of a white swan strengthens our confidence that this conclusion is true. However, should we come across one black swan then the inference would be falsified. The conclusion is therefore probably true, but not logically certain. This is in contrast to deductive reasoning which is not empirically based, but based wholly on logic. Here, if the premises are true, then the conclusions must also be true. An example of this is the classic argument: P1 – All men are mortal; P2 – Socrates is a man; C – Socrates is mortal. Philosophers have used several inductive arguments to try to prove the existence of God. The most famous of these have been the teleological argument (the argument for a designer) and the cosmological argument. These arguments use the evidence from the world and argue logically back to God. A classic deductive argument is the ontological argument for the existence of God. The OA, however, is difficult for most students below Year 12.

Pupils working at higher levels

- To discuss: Does induction or deduction tell us more about the world and the ways things are? What about God?

- Pupils could devise a quiz with examples called 'Is this inductive or deductive reasoning?'

- Inductive story: pupils could write a mystery story that ends with the conclusion that 'God exists'. This could be done as a useful summary of the traditional arguments for the existence of God. Some younger pupils may need help with the structure. See right column.

- Pupils could make a bank of evidence from things both man-made and from the natural world. They could play 'It's all a matter of evidence using this evidence. Is it possible to argue from anything back to God?

- Pupils can make up a story based on induction where the wrong conclusions were drawn, even though the evidence provided was fairly conclusive.

- Pupils could choose some simple practical science experiments to do in class to understand how inductive reasoning infers evidence from observations to make a generalised rule. http://pbskids.org/zoom/activities/sci/pendulumchallenge.html

Pupils working at lower levels

- As this game only requires imagination, pupils of all ages and abilities should be able to play it. However, some pupils may need extra time to construct answers and could find a planning frame useful. Some might find it useful to brainstorm the link between each piece of evidence and the scenario. If pupils are struggling they could write down how the scenario might have occurred first, and then try to slot the evidence in.

- Some students may need a starter sentence or writing frame for the creative story (see left column). It could go something like this:

  He was on the trail for God. But how did you detect an undetectable being? The first clue lay on the ground before him. He reached down and picked up a … 'Aha!' he said.

  The second clue came as he was writing up the first. He looked into the vast distance and saw … 'That's it!' he exclaimed.

Teacher's notes: 6. Could we be mistaken about all of our beliefs?

Suggested teaching activities

A11 The Great Deception

- Pupils to read about the new invention by Zapenflagen and the 'textbook' excerpt. Pupils should be aware that all our sensory data is carried as electro-chemical signals. Teachers may wish to flag this up – it is necessary to understand how Zapenflagen's invention works. Brains in vats need electro-chemical signals. These signals would have to accurately represent the coded electro-chemical signals of sense data. Although this does not seem remotely possible, analysing and recreating some chemical signals is. For example, there is a booming business in fake perfume that relies on analysing chemical signals from the original perfume accurately.)

- Pupils should then read the *History of the World Magazine* article and consider whether it is possible to know whether there currently are brains in vats.

- Pupils could walk to the school field and then back to a classroom where the field can no longer be seen. Students could discuss whether they know that the field still exists. Be prepared for a range of comments about this question!

- Dr Johnson answered the sceptic's challenge that we cannot know the real world (he was attacking Bishop Berkeley's defence of idealism at the time) by kicking a stone and famously quipping 'I refute it thus!' A teacher might like to do something similar in class and ask students whether the sceptic's challenge has been successfully overcome through that act, or whether it misses the point.

- Teachers may wish to raise with pupils the impact of the sceptic's challenge. If the challenge is successful, then does this affect daily life where we need to make constant assumptions about knowledge?

- An enjoyable way to explore this topic is by watching parts of *The Matrix* (cert 15), particularly the scenes when Neo finds out from Morpheus what the Matrix is, as it heavily relies on Descartes's evil demon scenario.

- Descartes believed that God's existence could save us from the evil demon argument. Pupils to work out how this might be the case.

Learning objectives and outcomes

To consider the sceptic's challenge that it is impossible to be certain about anything.

Synopsis

A11: A brain-in-a-vat scenario introduces the sceptic's challenge.

This story is based on Descartes's evil demon hypothesis (see below) and the modern 'brain-in-a-vat' scenarios developed in the 1950s.

Professor Zapenflagen has developed a way of prolonging life by placing disembodied brains in vats of nutrient-rich liquid. However, he must convince the brains that they are experiencing real life. Meanwhile Dr Meg Lomaniac has acquired the machine. How do we know that we are not all brains in a vat?

Religious literacy: Words to be introduced – scepticism, brain-in-a-vat. Words that could be introduced at a higher level – evil demon, *cogito ergo sum*.

Prior learning: None required.

Links: Video clips from *The Matrix* alongside philosophical articles about the brain-in-a-vat scenario can be found at http://whatisthematrix. warnerbros.com/rl_cmp/new_phil_fr_intro.html

For **Background**, see p. 19.

Pupils working at higher levels

- Pupils could research how the brain works www.howstuffworks.com/brain.htm

- Pupils could extend Descartes's thought experiment by trying to work out any tests they could do to see if they can deduce that they are not being tricked by an evil demon right now. If they cannot do this then how are they to solve the sceptic's challenge that we know virtually nothing?

- If we cannot trust our senses for knowledge about the world, then what can we trust? (Pupils could be introduced to Descartes's *cogito ergo sum* – I think therefore I am.)

- There are many ethical and religious questions that can be drawn from the brain-in-a-vat scenario, concerning sanctity of life. If this technology was available, is it ethically permissable?

- Pupils could be introduced to the sceptic's paradox (provided they understand what a paradox is). Scepticism claims that we cannot know anything . . . if this is so then we cannot know the sceptic's claim. If we do know it is true then we know at least one thing is true. If this is the case then we can know other things too.

Pupils working at lower levels

- *The Truman Show* (cert 12) addresses the question of whether we are being deceived in our everyday beliefs. In the film the character Christos (who created the show) quips, 'We accept the reality we are presented with.' To what extent is this true?

- Pupils to think about things that they were told by their parents or others when they were very young (Santa Claus, the tooth fairy, Easter bunny). Did they accept these readily? Why? At what stage did they stop believing? What was the cause of their beliefs changing? Did they come to conclusions by themselves? Or was the information revealed to them by others? If no one ever told them, then would they ever know differently? What conditions would need to be present in order to work out that the belief was not true? How do we know that we are not in that situation now?

Teacher's notes: Summary

Suggested teaching activities

- **Summary question** – *'Is it possible to gain knowledge of God? If so, how might we gain knowledge of God?'*

  After looking at the strengths and weaknesses of both the rationalist and the empiricist models for knowledge (A12), teachers can make the link with knowledge about God. In what ways can God be known? Is it mainly through rationalism, empiricism or something else (such as innate knowledge)? See *Truth-Seekers: Thinking about God*, **B1 Knowing God.**

  Teachers could discuss with pupils:
  - How knowledge about God is different from knowledge about things in the material world. (This is because things in the material world are tangible.)
  - Whether it is possible to have true knowledge of God, or whether, like Kierkegaard, there is a point where you have to take a leap of faith.

A12 Discussion grid: Can we know anything for sure?

- This grid, accompanied by **A13 Guidelines for group discussion**, can be used to facilitate focused small group discussions. Guidelines should first be discussed with a whole class. Then, in small groups (ideally four pupils per group), each member is given a focusing role (from the Guidelines). However, pupils should be aware that all members are expected to contribute with ideas. The group leader writes the initials of each member of the group in the top row, one column per group member. The group begin the guided discussion. Whenever a member contributes, the group leader will tick the relevant box. Teachers can collect these sheets to use as a focus for feedback/plenary, directing questions to those with ticks against their names.

  At the end of the discussion time, the teacher may like to collect the sheets and focus feedback on specific individuals who had a tick in the box alongside that question.

  At the end of the feedback, the groups might like to reflect on how well they work as a group/in their roles.

A14 Summary

The two boxes offer summary notes. The first is an A5-size summary of Knowledge that may be helpful revision for some pupils. It can be copied and stuck in an exercise book. There is also a list of key words for the unit. The list is not comprehensive and pupils can add to it.

Background to All: Descartes, in his Meditations, questions whether any of the things we commonly believe or know are grounded in certainty. He argues that as many of the things he once believed have turned out to be false, then could it not be the case that other things are false, or indeed, our whole world picture? Descartes begins this pursuit of certainty by arguing that our senses often give us unreliable information about the world. As most, if not all, of our beliefs have a common source in the senses, then we might be sceptical of all these beliefs that depend upon them. However, in general our senses are reliable and as such should be trusted overall. His next argument concerns our dreaming state. Sometimes when we vividly dream, we are convinced that the dream world is real. There are no adequate ways of individually distinguishing a sleep state from an awakened state. If this is the case, then we could doubt all our experiences. However, Descartes notes that this sceptical challenge does not succeed, as mathematical truths continue to hold in a dream state. Finally, he posits the evil demon hypothesis, from which modern brain-in-a-vat arguments are derived. This asks how we know

that we are not in the hands of an evil demon that has set out to deceive us, using all forms of power and illusion. Descartes answers his own challenge through his proofs for the existence of God. He also assumes that God, being perfect, would not deceive, as this is an imperfection. This is coupled with his clarity and distinctness criterion. This states: 'Whatever I clearly and distinctly perceive to be true is true.' Therefore, if we can prove that God exists, and our thoughts are carefully thought out, then our knowledge about the world can be taken to be correct. Some commentators have accused Descartes of a circular argument here. Moreover, Descartes's arguments for the existence of God (cosmological and ontological) have received criticism. If this is so then we will need to find a different solution to the sceptic's argument. (One such solution uses the private language argument by Hilary Putnam in *Reason, Truth and History*).

The brain-in-the-vat thought experiment is widely known and was developed from Descartes's evil demon argument.

A1 Fact, opinion, belief

Look at the following rant by a Neasden United supporter. She is arguing that Neasden United are not just her favourite team but are the best team.

Separate the **facts**, **opinions** and **beliefs** in this passage. Make sure you can back up your answers with reasons.

'Neasden United are the best team ever! We are much better than our rivals Arsenal United. Last year we won the Brent Cup and this year we even beat Wembley 3:1. We are doing so well that by 2015 we will have entered the 5th division. No one can stop us, we have seven victories this season under our belt.'

- What evidence would be needed to prove that Neasden United are the best team ever?

- What is the difference between an opinion and a belief?

Abdi is talking about stealing. How much of this is fact?

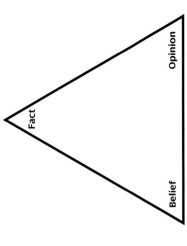

'Of course it is wrong to steal. Our law says that you can't steal. Most religions say that you shouldn't steal. People who steal things should be locked up, especially people who steal again and again. There were 100,000 robberies in London last year. However, occasionally there are good reasons for stealing, such as a poor person taking food for her family.'

- What are the beliefs and opinions in this passage?

What is religious knowledge?

- Look at the following statements. Are they facts, opinions or beliefs?
- Which ones are the most difficult to sort out (and why)?

> **Miracles happen.**
> **Hindus believe in reincarnation.**
> **Eating animals is wrong.**
> **Bowing your head when you pray helps you concentrate.**
> **Sam believes that God exists.**
> **The Bible is the holy book of Christians.**
> **There will be a judgement day.**
> **Murder is wrong.**
> **Muslims pray five times a day.**
> **Jesus lived 2000 years ago.**
> **Jesus was the son of God.**

A2 Separating fact from opinion

When we listen to others, we generally hear a mixture of facts, opinions and beliefs.

Sometimes it is hard to separate one from the other. Can you give a definition of a fact? What about an opinion? How is a belief different from facts and opinions?

Cut out the cards below. Can you separate them into three areas: fact, opinion and belief. Are there any cards that you think should be in more than one pile? Explain your answer.

Now take each pile and place them near the corresponding corner of the triangle below. Next, place each word somewhere along one side of the triangle. You will need to decide which side of the corner to place the word, depending on whether it is nearer fact/opinion, fact/belief or opinion/belief. Try to place each word in order with the words closest to fact, opinion or belief near the corners.

Thought	Feeling	Impression
Information	View	Judgement
Verified	Notion	Ruling
Proof	True	Sentiment
Knowledge	Reason	Trust

Fact

Opinion

Belief

Truth-Seekers: **Thinking about Truth**

A4 Ignorance log

> Not ignorance, but ignorance of ignorance, is the death of knowledge.
>
> (A. N. Whitehead)

What things am I ignorant of?
(In the box brainstorm all the things that you do not know, but would like to.)

I would like to find the answer to . . .
(Write down the one thing you would like to discover more about.)

In seeking the answer I will need more knowledge. I will need to find out . . . .
(What knowledge do you need?)

In seeking the answer I will need to ask these questions:
(Try to generate at least 10 questions.)

To get this knowledge I will . . .
(How will you get this knowledge?)

I have discovered . . .

Truth-Seekers: **Thinking about Truth**

A3 Quotes on knowledge

'The master said, "Tzu Lu, shall I teach you what knowledge is? When you know a thing, to recognise that you know it: and when you do not know a thing, to recognise that you do not know it. That is knowledge."'

Confucius

There will come a time when our descendants will be amazed that we did not know things that are so plain to them. . . . Our universe is a sorry little affair unless it has in it something for every age to investigate.

Seneca

Ideas are everywhere, but knowledge is rare.

Thomas Sowell

A man is but what he knows.

Francis Bacon

Not ignorance, but ignorance of ignorance, is the death of knowledge.

A. N. Whitehead

Only when we know a little do we know anything; doubt grows with knowledge.

Goethe

Nothing in all the world is more dangerous than sincere ignorance and conscientious stupidity.

Martin Luther King

Nothing that is worth knowing can be taught.

Oscar Wilde

Every man takes the limits of his own field of vision for the limits of the world.

Arthur Schopenhauer

You do not really understand something unless you can explain it to your grandmother.

Albert Einstein

Knowledge that does not generate achievement is a pale and bloodless thing, unworthy of mankind.

Will Durant

We do not know a truth without knowing its cause.

Aristotle

Where there is shouting there is no true knowledge.

Leonardo da Vinci

We sometimes get all the information, but we refuse to get the message.

Cullen Hightower

The difference between what the most and the least learned people know is inexpressibly trivial in relation to that which is unknown.

Albert Einstein

I know, Meno, what you mean. You argue that a man cannot inquire either about that which he knows, or about that which he does not know; for if he knows, he has no need to inquire; and if not, he cannot; for he does not know that very subject about which he is to inquire.

Socrates

A6   How knowledgeable are the Zarg?

It was time for the Zarg to send another report home. Zarg on the home planet were keen to share their knowledge about earth . . .

Zarg Report no.13   98.1/74/500089
EARTH CREATURES

We believe that humans are like birds (see Report 12). Our evidence for this is that every year many humans in cold countries, such as the UK, migrate to warmer climates. We believe that many humans play a game called football. Our evidence is that many people wear football clothing in the streets. Some humans like eating a substance called honey. We have discovered where honey comes from. We believe it comes from bees (see Report 9). Our evidence for this is that honey is yellow and bees are also yellow. We believe that many humans love working. They spend more time at work than they do at home. While they wear casual clothes at home, they show they care about work more by dressing up in their best clothes. We believe that some humans keep other humans as pets. These human-pets are kept in a black box in the corner of their room. The humans often gaze as their human pets perform and even shout at them.

We believe that humans need air to survive. We took one as a sample to send home to you and locked it in an airtight container to keep him fresh. Unfortunately the sample soon died. We will keep continuing our efforts to obtain a live sample for you . . .

The Zarg have certainly been very attentive in their observations. They have used their reasoning skills and have backed up each conclusion with evidence. However, have they drawn the correct conclusions about earth?

- What do the Zarg mean by human pets?
- How have the Zarg come to these conclusions?
- On the basis of Report 13, do you think that the Zarg know anything about earth at all?
- Write down any real knowledge the Zarg have gained about earth.
- Write down any true beliefs the Zarg have that do not amount to knowledge.
- Write down any justified beliefs that the Zarg have that do not amount to knowledge.

A5   What is knowledge?

We claim to know many things. I know that 2 + 3 = 5. Joon claims to know that Wellington is the capital of New Zealand. Carly says that she knows God exists. Joseph says he knows that Chelsea are the best football team. Can we say that they have true knowledge of these things? How can we tell the difference between a belief and knowledge?

Rakesh believes that there are little green aliens on the planet Zig. Rakesh has no evidence to back this up. He believes it because of the popular film *Aliens from Zig*.

- In 200 years from now, scientists discover that there is a planet (which they name Zig, after the film) with little green aliens inhabiting it.
  Would we say that Rakesh *knew* that the aliens lived on Zig?

No. He had a belief that turned out to be true, but had no evidence to back up his belief.

A **true belief** by itself is not enough for knowledge.

LONG LANE COMMUNITY SCHOOL

NEWSLETTER

Dear Parents and Guardians,

Please note that the school will be closed from 17 February until 25 February for the half-term holiday.

Can we take this opportunity to remind you not to park on the double-yellow lines outside the school

Sameena believes that tomorrow is the start of the holidays. She is justified in believing that because her school newsletter said that the holiday would begin on 17 February and today is 16 February.

Would we say that Sameena *knows* that tomorrow is the start of the holiday? It looks like she does. She has evidence to back up her belief. However, we do not know if her belief is true. As it happened, the school printed the wrong holiday dates and Sameena will have to come into school tomorrow.

A **justified belief** by itself is not enough for knowledge.

Some philosophers claim that for knowledge we need **justified, true belief.**

- Write down ten things that you believe.
- How many of these things can you know for certain?
- For each belief, say whether it is true, and your justification (good reasons) for believing it.

A7 How well do you know your stuff?

Instructions

How well do you think you know things?

Look at the list below. For each thing, mark it on a scale of 0–10.

0 is something that you do not know at all (you do not know what it is or have not heard of it).

10 is something that you know extremely well. You have almost perfect knowledge about it.

Next to each mark you place on the scale, write a couple of sentences to explain HOW well you know the thing.

(For example, I know my Aunty Marjorie lives in Stanmore because my mum told me, even though I have not visited her yet.)

1 Spaghetti bolognese

2 Oliver Twist

3 New Zealand

4 London

5 Your bed

6 2 + 2 = 4

7 Prime Minister

8 Football

9 The wind is blowing outside the room.

10 Tables

I know this extremely well — 10

9

8

7

6

I know something about this — 5

4

3

2

1

I do not know this at all — 0

A8 How do we gain our knowledge?

Everyone accepts that we all know a lot of things. However, people have debated *how* we have come to know all the things we do. We learn many things about the world through experience. Think about a young baby exploring her environment.

How does she learn that carpets are not for eating but dinners are?
How does she learn that doors have hard edges but cushions are soft?

Most of our knowledge comes from the experiences we have from our senses.

* Write down some things that a baby will learn in the first two years of life. Underline those things that are learned through our senses.

We also learn many things about the world through working things out.

* What have you learned through reasoning today?

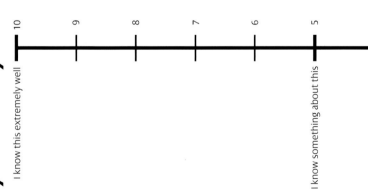

* Brainstorm as many facts about the world as you can.
* Look through your list. For each example say *how* you know it is true.
* Which examples are known through rationalism?
* Which examples are known through empiricism?

Which of the following

* Divide the following statements into ones that you can discover rationally, and those that you can discover empirically. Are there any that you are unsure about?

a) The train is due to arrive at 8.15 a.m.

b) The train due at 8.15 a.m. is late!

c) My best friend's sister's friend is the cousin of the manager of Coldplay.

d) I don't know enough for my Geography test tomorrow!

e) The three corners of a triangle always add up to 180 degrees.

f) She knows that she gets the twins mixed up.

g) 1, 3, 7, 11, 13, 17 are all prime numbers.

René Descartes

A rationalist is someone who believes that we gain knowledge about the world through **reason** and not experience.

All that I have accepted as certain I have learned from the senses; but it is sometimes proved to me that the senses are deceptive, and it is wiser not to trust entirely to any thing by which we have once been deceived.

John Locke

An empiricist is someone who believes that we gain knowledge about the world through **experience.**

To this I answer, in one word, from experience, in that all our knowledge is founded.

(23)

A9 Can our senses deceive us?

Hearing

- Can you identify sounds as well as you think you can?

- In pairs try out this test. Person 1 blindfolds person 2. Person 1 then makes 10 different noises in turn. Person 2 has to try to identify the noise. Person 1 writes down each answer.

You could use some of these noises:
1 Clap your hands.
2 Open a zipped pencil case.
3 Shut a hardback book loudly.
4 Squeak a marker on the whiteboard.
5 Stamp your feet.
6 Rustle some papers.
7 Drop some pens on the table.
8 Close the door.
9 Staple a piece of paper.
10 Brush your hair.

Smell

- Can you identify smells as well as you think you can?

- In pairs try out this test. Person 2 blindfolds person 1. Person 2 hands five containers with smells inside them to person 1. Person 1 tries to identify each smell. Person 2 writes down each answer.

You must use some strong-smelling objects for this test. The objects must be kept separate so their smells do not mix.

You could use:
1 Herbs such as rosemary or mint.
2 Pine needles.
3 Lemon.
4 Strawberries.
5 Orange peel.
6 Chocolate.
7 Coffee.
8 Vinegar (salt and vinegar crisps will do).
9 Perfume.
10 Pencil shavings.

Touch

- Can you identify textures as well as you think you can?

- In pairs try out this test. Person 2 blindfolds person 1. Person 2 hands various things to person 1 to identify. Person 2 records the answers of person 1.

You could use some of these textures:
1 Furry material.
2 Silky material.
3 A smooth stone.
4 Wood.
5 Metal.
6 Plastic.
7 A shoe.

Or, person 1 should try to identify different body parts without sight. You could use a shoulder, nose, knee, hand, head, foot or elbow.

Or person 1 could place their hands in hot then cold water and then in hot water again. This second time round, do they record their answer as hot or not?

Taste

- Can you identify tastes as well as you think you can?

- In pairs try out this test. Person 1 blindfolds person 2. Person 2 should hold their nose for all tests. Person 1 feeds a jellybean to person 2 to taste. Person 1 records the flavour of jellybean before person 2 answers, and then person 2's answer.

- Jellybeans are good to use as they have a similar texture but different flavours. Other sweets could be substitutes.

- Some people cannot differentiate between apples and pears without their sense of smell. However, if using these fruits, make sure the pear is not of a grainy texture.

A10 It's all a matter of evidence

Aim

This game uses reasoning to reach a solution. Use your creative intelligence to work out what might have happened.

Instructions

Each group should get a pack of cards. The evidence cards should be printed on a different colour to the scenario cards. The cards should be pre-cut and in an envelope. There is an empty template for scenarios and evidence.

1 Each group of four must at random take one scenario card and then three evidence cards.

2 Work out what must have happened to cause the scenario using only the evidence available. (The evidence *must* be integral to the induction). Additional characters may be added.

3 One person should be the leader, responsible for ensuring that everyone has given an opinion, and for governing the selection process for the solution.

4 Answers should be recorded on the template sheet (A10 continued).

Scenario cards	Evidence cards	Evidence cards	Evidence cards
Jemima was lying face down on the floor, unconscious.	A cooker	A feather	Scissors
The ship stopped in the middle of the sea, stranding the passengers.	Animal tracks	A chair	A manual on fixing cars
The Moolah Bank had been broken into.	A rotten smell	A book	Footprints
Philip looked into his bag. His mobile phone had gone!	Charcoal	A pen	A watch
The school fire alarm had gone off again!	A book in another language	A saucepan	A compass
Bob rolled over in his bed, clutching his stomach.	A car	A knife	A loud bang
Jemima shouted out, 'NO!'	A jumper	A needle	A fishing rod
Sld had got into the premiere of the new movie *Bighit*.	A dog	A spoon	A video-case
'AVALANCHE!'	An eraser	Blood stains	A pair of net curtains

A10 continues

A11 The Great Deception

Professor Zapenflagen was working on his latest medical discovery. This would revolutionise the world! He had worked on this for the last 30 years: a way to keep people alive for up to 60 years longer! He called his invention the Zapovat™. His reasoning was simple. People's bodies tended to yield to old age. Eventually the human body wears out or goes wrong. The solution was evident! Get rid of the body parts and focus on the brain! He had finally worked out a way for the brain to be sealed into a vat of nutrient-rich liquid. This would keep the brain healthy. The problem was that a brain in a vat was not connected to anything. He had given his test brains a blood supply and oxygen. However, as yet the brains could not experience the world. So, he consulted his neuroscience textbook. . . .

History of the World
Magazine   Year 2090

The 1995 Great Deception

Zapenflagen won the Nobel prize for his discovery in 1991. Oh, such good intentions! But good intentions can go awry. After Zapenflagen's invention was heralded in the journal *Nature World*, everyone wanted to see it work. Zapenflagen received many offers for the Zapovat™. The highest bid was from a rather rich Dr Meg Lomaniac.

Zapenflagen unwittingly sold the machine to Lomaniac, who had a dastardly plan. She was not going to use the Zapovat™ to extend life, she was going to use it to control life! If she could control people then she would have access to their fortunes! By 1985 Meg Lomaniac had hundreds of thousands of brains bottled and preserved in a vat. They were none the wiser. The Great Deception, as it is now referred to, lasted until the year 2020 when Lomaniac was overthrown.

Neuroscience Today

BRAIN FACTS

Your brain collects and interprets the information received from your senses. Without your brain you could not think, imagine or reason. Without your brain you would not have physical or emotional feelings. Our brain controls ALL of our senses. When we feel, smell, hear, taste something, it is because millions of nerves are carrying an electrical message to our brain.

Ahhh! Professor Zapenflagen saw what he had to do. That afternoon, armed with wires and crocodile clips, he connected the brain's neurons by wires to an amazingly sophisticated computer. He provided the brain with electrical impulses which were identical to the ones the brain usually received every day.

'I shall suppose then that there is, not a true God, but a certain evil demon, who is clever and deceitful as he is powerful, and who has employed all his energies to deceive me. I shall consider that the sky, the air, the earth, colours, shapes and sounds . . . are nothing but illusions and tricks.'

René Descartes asked how we know anything for sure. After all, our senses often fail us, and sometimes we dream we are awake while we are asleep. Descartes asked us to imagine that an evil demon has tricked us into thinking there is a world. Everything we see and feel is just an illusion. Even maths and physics are things made up by him. How would we know whether the demon is tricking us?

How do you know you are not a brain-in-a-vat?

A10 It is all a matter of evidence *(continued)*

It's all a matter of solutions

Scenario	Evidence 1	Evidence 2	Evidence 3

Record all the solutions your group suggests below. Highlight the solution that you think is the most convincing.

1

2

3

4

Can you think of any evidence that might be used to prove the existence of God?

A12 Discussion grid

Can we know anything for sure?

Use this grid to help your group to discuss effectively. Follow the questions. Tick a box when a person from your group has spoken. Starred questions should be answered by each person in your group.

Initials of group members (one set of initials per column)				
*Give examples of things that you are sure that you know.				
Do you know them through reason or experience?				
*What makes you so sure that you really KNOW these things and not just BELIEVE these things?				
Give an example of a time when your senses have deceived you.				
Give an example of a time when your reasoning was wrong.				
Summarise the points made so far by the group.				
(Now everyone needs to write the summarised points in their books.)				
What makes you so sure that you have not made a mistake this time?				
Is it *in theory* possible that you could have made a mistake this time?				
'Give the views of at least one philosopher on this topic.				
*Revise your initial comments if necessary: What things are you SURE that you know?				
*Come to a group consensus on the question 'What can we know?' Write down your final answer and explain why you have agreed this as a group. What arguments did your group reject and why did they reject them?				

A13 Guidelines for group discussion

- **Listen!**
  Good listening is essential for discussions. You will come out with better ideas if you listen first and then think about how to reply.

- **Take turns!**
  Discussions are more interesting if everybody takes part. You will also benefit from different viewpoints.

- **Question each other!**
  Don't take what people say at face value. Probe into people's reasons for holding an opinion. Has the speaker thought about the question before speaking?

- **Think and then talk!**
  Think things through before you answer.

- **Have fun!**
  Discussions and debates can be fun. Make sure that yours is. Don't make anyone feel bad for stating an opinion. Be polite. Respect people's reasons for holding an opinion, even if you disagree with them. A bit of humour in a discussion helps!

Listening skills

Listen carefully.
* Has the speaker given reasons?
* What evidence is there to support what the speaker is saying?
* Is the speaker stating a fact, an opinion or a belief?

Questioning skills

Question each other to further your investigations.
* Try asking these questions:
  What is the question asking us?
  What do you mean by that?
  Can you give us an example?
  What has this to do with our question?
* When questioning, don't ask personal questions, or put people on the spot.

Talking skills

Give yourself some thinking time before you contribute.
* Put across your point clearly.
* Make sure that you do not offend anyone.
* Can you back up what you are saying?
* Try to anticipate responses to your point.
* Don't be afraid to change your mind!

Leading a group

* Try to keep the discussion focused on the issue.
* Make sure that no one dominates the discussion.
* Is everybody giving opinions and answering questions?

A14 Summary

Key words

Belief – A reasoned judgement which is held as true.

Fact – Information which can be proved to be true.

Opinion – A personal feeling or view that is not based on certainty.

Knowledge – Justified true belief.

Experience – Knowledge that is gained through directly participating in an activity.

Evidence – Your basis for believing or not believing something.

Rationalism – The view that we cannot gain true knowledge of the world through experience.

Empiricism – The view that all our knowledge about the world comes through experience, but through reason.

Induction – A method of reasoning where the truth of the conclusion is probable, based on observations and empirical evidence.

Deduction – A method of reasoning where the conclusion is logically drawn from the premises.

Knowledge

Many religions claim to have knowledge about God. The problem is that many of these claims appear to contradict each other. For example, Christians believe that there is only one God, while some Hindus believe that there are many gods. Many religions claim to know what happens when you die. Many Buddhists and Hindus believe that you will be reincarnated on earth, depending on how you lived your life. Many Christians and Muslims believe that you go to heaven or hell depending on your actions on earth. Not all these beliefs can be literally true!

The question of how we gain knowledge is important. Some people think that we gain knowledge only through experience. Some think that knowledge can only arise from reason, while others think that it is a mixture of experience and reason.

I think that we gain knowledge through ....

because ....

The problem with knowing God through experience is that sometimes our senses can let us down and we might be mistaken in what we see or hear. The problem with knowing God through reason is that sometimes our reasoning can be faulty.

Another important question is how do we *know* that we have knowledge about God, rather than a belief about God?

Many Hindus claim that when we die we are reincarnated. Is this a belief or is it knowledge?
What would we need to show in order to prove that it is knowledge?

Unit B Arguing effectively

About the unit

This unit suggests activities and support material to aid pupils in making and evaluating logical arguments. Almost all religious groups make truth claims. As well as examining claims to truth, we need to see if claims are logical, whether they rely on emotive language or if they are dependent on previous assumptions.

The ability to argue in a logical and effective manner is essential in RE. In all A Level and GCSE RS specifications, students are tested on their ability to make both balanced and evaluative arguments. This topic is best taught alongside religious or ethical issues, so that pupils can make informed judgements.

Where this unit fits in

This unit links with the following Key Stage 3 guidelines in the non-statutory national framework for RE:

• Learning about religion: 1d, 1e, 1f, 1g
• Learning from religion: 2a, 2e
• Religions and beliefs: 3a, 3d (adaptable for 3b)
• Themes: Is applicable from 3e to 3l
• Experiences and opportunities: 3o, 3p

This unit would help to prepare pupils for later GCSE work in RS by developing their ability for independent critical thinking, and consideration of the concepts of proof.

Attitudes in the unit

This unit helps pupils develop the following four attitudes outlined in the non-statutory national framework for RE:

Self awareness Feeling confident about their own beliefs and identity and sharing them with others without fear of embarrassment or ridicule, *e.g. articulating and reflecting critically on their own religious, philosophical and moral beliefs.*

Respect for all Being prepared to recognise and acknowledge their own bias, *e.g. when considering counter-objections to claims that the pupil made initially.*

Open-mindedness Distinguishing between opinions, viewpoints and beliefs in connection with issues of conviction and faith, *e.g. in examining how knowledge is different from belief.*

Appreciation and wonder Developing their imagination and curiosity, *e.g. by asking questions about puzzling aspects of life and moral and religious issues through ignorance logging.*

Learning objectives and outcomes

Pupils will learn one possible structure of a strong argument. They will give thought to possible objections and counter-objections to a given question. They will evaluate arguments, considering many factors including the grounding of reasons. They also will look at some common flaws in arguments. These include citing a false expert and the use of presenting only selective information to make a case. Pupils will make a creative attempt to find solutions to problems based on inductive reasoning and empirical evidence.

At lower levels: pupils will have made some basic arguments with supporting reasons. They will understand that our reasons are grounded and some grounds are better than others.

At higher levels: pupils will look at what makes a valid and true argument. They will study some common religious arguments and comment on whether they are sound in logic (and to what extent that matters). They might wish to test the validity of syllogisms using Venn diagrams.

Assessment example

Pupils could study a religious or ethical issue, and after using the argument tutorial, use the arguing templates if needed (**B3 Argument wall** for levels 3–5 and **B2 Argument builder** for levels 6–7) to help them to structure a response. Depending on the question chosen pupils will be able to show many skills, including: research, identification of relevant material, explanation, connecting ideas, analysis, evaluation and using a wide religious and philosophical vocabulary.

Examples of questions:
'Does God exist?' (Focus on the teleological argument and the cosmological argument.)
'Are creation and evolution compatible?' (Studying Genesis 1, religious language and evolution.)
'What happens when we die?' (Looking at Hindu and Muslim concepts of the afterlife.)
'Why do we have pain and evil if God is good?' (After studying the problem of evil.)
'The aim of life is to be happy. Discuss.' (Studying Buddhism, Humanism and Christianity.)
'Do we have a duty to help others?' (With a focus on Sikhism and the concept of sewa.)

Level 4: Pupils will express some religious ideas and beliefs in response to the question and explain what they mean. Pupils will use some religious/philosophical vocabulary appropriately, and give a personal opinion.

Level 5: Pupils will make an informed response to the question with supporting points and some reference to a different point of view. They will use some religious/philosophical vocabulary in an appropriate manner.

Level 6: Pupils will use reasoning and examples to answer the question. They will attempt to explain both sides of the argument and conclude with an informed personal response. They will use relevant philosophical and religious terms.

Level 7: Pupils will effectively evaluate religious and non-religious views in response to the question, using appropriate examples. They will give an informed personal response. Pupils will use a wide religious/philosophical vocabulary.

Level 8: Pupils will weigh up in detail a wide range of religious and world-views in answer to the question. Pupils will use a comprehensive religious/philosophical vocabulary. Answers will be logically argued, will include explanations and examples, and a personal opinion. There will be a suitably informed conclusion.

Useful background resources

Teacher books: *The Miniature Guide to Critical Thinking: Concepts & Tools* – Richard Paul and Linda Elder
Critical Thinking – Brooke Moore and Richard Parker

Websites: www.criticalthinking.org.uk – Useful site geared to the OCR AS critical thinking specification.
www.criticalthinking.org – The Foundation for Critical Thinking has useful resources available.

Religious literacy

Through the activities in this unit pupils will understand, use and spell correctly the following words and terms: *analysis, argument, bias, claim, evaluation, false expert, ground, interpretation, objection/counter-objection, premise, syllogism.*

Index of key questions and related activity sheets

Note: **core activities are listed in bold**; *extension activities are listed in italic.*

Teacher's notes: 1. How do you build a strong argument?

Suggested teaching activities

B1 Building arguments

There are many ways to build an argument. This is one visual method that pupils can use to aid making arguments. Although the templates appear prescriptive, pupils should be encouraged to use them only as models and should have as many branches as they can/are appropriate.

- The wall-building analogy aids pupils in thinking about things to consider when making arguments. Teachers can draw out the importance of each part of the analogy by asking questions, e.g.:
  - What would happen if there was no cement in a wall?
  - What happens if the argument and reasons are not connected properly?
  - What would happen if a bricklayer placed bricks in a random order?
  - What would happen if we placed parts of an argument in a random order?

- Pupils could begin by making an argument equivalent of a 'bag of cement'; a set of connecting words that they could use when connecting reasons/evidence to the claim and the objections to the reasons/evidence.

Teachers may wish to give the following examples: 'On the other hand'; 'I believe this because'; 'The reasons I have for this are . . .'.

- Pupils should make their way through the tutorial-style worksheets. They should start at the centre of a clean page (A4 or ideally **A3**). The subject matter is the existence of God. However, this can be substituted for any issue that pupils have been studying.

Before they tackle the first sheet, pupils could brainstorm in groups reasons for believing in God. The emphasis here should be on quantity of reasons and not quality (see page 5, Extended brainstorming rules).

Each stage of the sheet adds another stage of building an argument. By Stage 4 they should have mapped out a fair argument. Pupils should be encouraged to add more reasons than just the two given. **B6** follows on from the end of **B1**.

- If pupils need more practice at mapping their arguments, they could use the template sheet **B2 Argument builder**. The purpose of this frame is to familiarise pupils with making comprehensive arguments. This template sheet would benefit from being photocopied onto A3 to give pupils more room to write. Note that the argument builder frame also aids pupils in evaluating arguments. Evaluation should only be carried out when pupils have covered grounding reasons.

- Different pupils will appreciate different ways of seeing the connections within their thinking and writing. There are two other evaluation planning sheets (see **B4 Arguing frames**): the pie frame and the evaluation planning frame. The circle structure of the pie frame encourages pupils to make their point succinctly, then gradually expand with their detail. The middle line is accentuated so that pupils may use this as a template for both for and against arguments. The frame should preferably be enlarged to A3.

The evaluation planning frame sheet also needs to be enlarged to A4 size. This frame helps GCSE pupils structure their answers for an examination evaluation question. This gives pupils practice at writing from a balanced, neutral perspective as distinct from giving their own perspective.

Learning objectives and outcomes

To learn how to structure an argument.

Synopsis

B1: Looks at the structures that make a good argument.

Building a strong wall requires lots of bricks and a structure to hold it in place.

Argument building also requires lots of 'bricks' and a strong structure so that the result is strong.

Pupils working at higher levels

- Pupils could develop other metaphors for argument building (e.g. tree development/ construction site/jigsaw).

- Pupils could try to make as long an argument chain as possible, using the following formula: premise – reason – objection – counter-objection, and then as many following objections to that as possible. The longest ones could be displayed on cards around the room.

- In groups pupils could make a wall frieze to demonstrate how arguments are constructed. Each group could focus on a particular argument (e.g. the existence of God; the problem of evil and suffering).

- Pupils could look through newspaper articles to identify the grounds of knowledge and assess their strength.

- Pupils could use the scaffolds in **B4 Arguing frames** to help structure essays, enabling them to summarise points succinctly and provide a suitable level of supporting detail/evidence.

Pupils working at lower levels

- Pupils might benefit from the structured sheet **B3 Argument wall** to aid their planning of an argument. This would benefit from being photocopied onto A3. This contains no evaluation at this stage. If pupils have more than two initial reasons, then pupils can stick sheets together, perhaps in a square with the central premise in the centre.

- Pupils can practise making their own arguments, or they can practise disassembling established arguments into the respective 'bricks'.

- To help pupils get used to the structure of an argument they could unscramble parts of the argument and place them in the argument wall. Examples used should correlate to the work pupils have been doing recently and can be taken from pupils' essays.

For example:
  - I believe that the miracle reported in the newspaper actually happened.
  - Newspapers can be wrong or biased.
  - However, this newspaper always reports stories as accurately as possible.

- Some pupils may need to begin at a more basic level by considering arguments that could be used for and against an issue. Pupils might start by sorting muddled arguments on the cards on sheet **B5 Big points and little points.**

Teacher's notes: 1. How do you build a strong argument?

Suggested teaching activities

B6 Grounding reasons

- Pupils to read through the sheet. These grounding reasons can be supplemented by extra examples from pupils.
- Pupils to look at a set of reasons (from the argument builder, or any other argument). In each case state what the grounds for the reason are.

Rank the grounds so the strongest ground is at the top and the weakest ground is at the bottom.

Pupils could do a spider diagram detailing the strengths and weaknesses for each ground of knowledge.

- Pupils to identify grounds for the objections and counter-objections.
- Pupils to fill in the table, finding examples of strong and weak grounds of knowledge.
- Pupils could do role plays in groups to illustrate both strong and weak grounds of knowledge. Each group should have a different ground of knowledge to work with (except logical, which if correct is always strong).
- Once pupils have grasped what makes a strong or weak grounding of a reason then they could go on to grade their reasons from 0 to 10 (10 proving the reason and 0 adding nothing to the reason).

To help them do this they can use the scale on **B7 Evaluation scale**. This could be used as a whole class tool, for individuals to draw on, or by a small group using the pointer.

- As an extension, pupils could redraft their arguments to make them as strong as possible.
- Pupils can now complete their argument builder template sheet (**B2**) and evaluate the

Learning objectives and outcomes

To identify grounds for reasons.

To evaluate which grounds are strongest, giving reasons why.

Synopsis

B6: Looks at what grounds our reasons.

Evaluating reasons is easier to accomplish if we know what has grounded those reasons in the first place.

Religious literacy: Words to be introduced – premise, claim, argument, conclusion, objection, counter-objection, ground, empirical, logic. Words that could be introduced at a higher level – analytic statement (a tautology), synthetic (a statement that can be empirically proven).

Prior learning: None necessary.

Links: Logic, philosophy, English.

Pupils working at higher levels

- Pupils to think of any other categories of things that ground our reasons.
- Pupils could take a magazine interview of a famous person and work out the grounds for the reasons they give in the interview.

They could then evaluate the reasons and suggest how the arguments made might be made stronger.

- Pupils to discuss the following: what is the strongest argument for the existence of God? What would make this argument stronger? What would be the strongest grounds for the reasons? Is it possible in reality to have a watertight argument for God's existence? Why or why not?

Pupils working at lower levels

- Pupils can test how well they understand **B6 Grounding reasons** with the help sheet **B8 Reasons for reasons**.

Pupils have to work out what the grounds of each quote is.

Radiohead are brilliant – Testimony
The new film – Expert
Potatoes – Personal
The booked train – Common knowledge
Gut feeling – Credibility
Biology lesson – Logical/expert
Maths lesson – Logical
The tomato-stained shirt – Empirical
Dinosaur bones – Expert
Weighing it up – Common knowledge

Note that some of these are harder than others (e.g. the Biology lesson, which is a tautology).

In particular it should be made clear to pupils that this exercise is just to find the grounding of the reason. The quality of some of these reasons is not the focus.

- If pupils have accomplished this easily then they could go on to evaluate each reason.

Background: It is essential that pupils evaluate conclusions of arguments. However, for this to be effective, we first have to evaluate the premise. Sometimes a valid argument can be made whose premises are false. By taking a closer look at our premises, we can check assumptions have not been made. For example, one reason a student might give to why some people believe in God might be outlined as follows: (1) The world exists, and (2) The world could not have created itself. Therefore the world needed a creator, and we call that creator God. While this is a good reason for the existence of God (it is the basis of the cosmological arguments), we need to ask on what basis do we accept the premises 'the world exists' and that 'the world needs a creator'? The first premise we can deal with easily; our grounds for believing this premise is the empirical evidence around us. We have the testimony of ourselves and of others that the world independently exists. It is also common knowledge that the world exists. The second premise is more difficult. How do we know that the claim, 'The world needs a creator' is true? There are seven main grounds that we might appeal to: personal testimony, testimony of others, expert opinion, common knowledge, empirical evidence, logic, and plausibility and credibility. This claim cannot yet be verified empirically, and seems to rest upon expert opinion. Some experts who are particularly knowledgeable about the earth believe that the universe could be eternal; others disagree and claim that something cannot come from nothing. In turn we might look at the grounds these experts have in believing this. We might also look at whether the expert is really an expert in cosmology or logic, whether the expert is uncompromised in her research, and the extent to which other experts conflict with her judgement.

Teacher's notes: 2. How can we evaluate an argument?

Suggested teaching activities

B9 Evaluating arguments

- Pupils to read the first half of the sheet and in groups consider the questions asked.

What are these people experts in?

This question is not as straightforward as it might appear. Most of the people in this list are well known for acting. However, probing a bit deeper, we get a fuller picture. Tom Hanks is a member of the National Space Society and was a national spokesperson for the WWII memorial campaign. Oprah Winfrey is probably the most interesting case to discuss. She is a well-known chat show host, has been ranked high in lists of influential people and is a well-known philanthropist. (See Background for more information.) Therefore, pupils may wish to research/have extra information about these celebrities in order to discuss where their expertise lies. The question of what makes an expert' is also relevant to this discussion.

What are the skills that are important in ruling a country?

Pupils could brainstorm this in small groups for five minutes and feed-back to a class discussion. The class could come to a consensus.

In what ways might these famous people be termed experts on these areas?

In small groups, pupils to make a judgement based on the previous two questions, backing up their answers with reasons.

Are you more or less likely to support a politician if a famous person supports them? Why?

Pupils should give their own response, backed up with reasons. After this, pupils should try to articulate what argument is being made through having these celebrities support Barack Obama as a presidential candidate. Then pupils can evaluate the argument.

- Pupils to discuss whether the argument goes further than this:

P1: These celebrities are skilled in their field, well known, well loved and influential with Americans.
P2: These celebrities are endorsing Barack Obama's campaign.
C: Therefore if these well loved and trusted celebrities are endorsing Obama's campaign, then we should trust their judgement and support him too.

To assess whether we should trust the evidence of a claim that rests upon a person's endorsement, pupils should ask (at least) the following three questions:

– Are they generally trustworthy in character?
– Are they a genuine expert in the area?
– Do they have conflicting interests?

- TV or radio adverts could be recorded and played back to the pupils. Pupils could analyse them for any evidence of the false expert argument. They should try to use the questions above to help them. Their answers could be placed in a table.

Learning objectives and outcomes

To identify and understand where a false expert argument is being used.

Synopsis

B9: Looks at the 'false expert' argument. We are exposed to arguments everywhere. This is especially so with the media. However, how can we tell if the arguments are strong or weak? Many arguments in the media use endorsements by other people, largely celebrities. However, does that endorsement really support the argument?

Religious literacy: Words to be introduced – argument, evidence, evaluation, conclusion, false expert argument.

Prior learning: None necessary.

Links: English.

Pupils working at higher levels

- Pupils could bring in magazines and find as many expert arguments as they can. They could cut out examples and make a class display, differentiating the true experts from the false experts and giving reasons. (They should refer to the questions on the left to help them decide.)

- Pupils could be given examples of arguments that rest on expert claims, and analyse them.

- Pupils could look at the following quotes and decide if they are guilty of the false expert argument:

'When the solution is simple, God is answering.' (Albert Einstein)

'The purpose of all war is ultimately peace.' (St Augustine)

- Pupils will need to think very carefully about their area of expertise and whether this makes their claims in this instance stronger or not.

Pupils working at lower levels

- Pupils could use the supplementary sheet *B10 Whose opinion should I trust?* The aim of the sheet is to help pupils think about why they trust some testimonies and not others. They are asked to match the experts' notes to the correct expert.
There is potential for some debate about what makes an expert, but more importantly, time could be taken to discuss stereotypes. The stereotypes on this page were chosen to represent common media examples. However, it is important to highlight that experts in all areas can be very different from expectations.

- This exercise could be extended by asking pupils to analyse whether each expert has a genuine expertise in the area; what area they have expertise in; and what are the conflicting interests that could arise in each situation.

- Pupils could work on making claims and giving reasons for those claims. They should then evaluate the claims on the evaluation sliding scale (see *B7 Evaluation scale*).

Background: We are often exposed to false expert arguments. This is particularly true in advertising where a celebrity backs up a claim. If a claim is to be successfully assessed on the basis of the opinion of an authority or expert, we would expect that expert to (a) be trustworthy in nature; (b) have no conflict of interests in the affirmation of the claim; (c) have a genuine proficiency, knowledge and skill in the area. The problem arises where the authority is not a genuine expert.
While I might be influenced by a respected actor's recommendation of films in a similar genre, I may not accept a recommendation from him if he was recommending live theatre (unless I knew of his expertise in this area). The issue that arises here is whether these celebrities' successes and experiences in their fields has given them genuine expertise in government. Oprah Winfrey is more than just an American chat show host. In several media lists she has been dubbed as one of the most powerful and influential women in the world. In a CNN/ *Time* '2001 Global Influentials' list she was dubbed arguably the world's most powerful woman'. In a 2007 *American Spectator* article she was also called 'arguably the most influential woman in the world'. This influence extends to recommendations she makes on her show. Her book-club selections make immediate best-sellers and this has become known as the 'Oprah Effect'. She is also a well-known philanthropist and has set up her own charity.

Teacher's notes: 3. Do we always look at different points of view?

Suggested teaching activities

B11 Half the story

The selective information argument
- Pupils should look at the advert for Greaser's crisps and answer the questions on the sheet.

The main argument is that buying (and by implication eating) Greaser's crisps will aid your health (through gaining fitness equipment).
The Branflakes advert is similar. While the advert highlights the beneficial ingredients, it neglects the fact that Branuflakes are high in salt, sugar and fat.
The fox advert neglects the issue of fox over-population and damage done to the chicken population.
The diabetes advert neglects the issue of animal testing.

- Pupils could think of a time where they saw things from only one point of view; or when they gave/received selective information.

This topic can be linked successfully to moral issues.

B12 Goldilocks behind bars

The story is clearly written from the bears' point of view, with evidence of bias and lots of emotive language. Pupils should be reminded of the concept of bias before proceeding.

Possible reasons for Goldilocks' actions could include:
She could have a medical disorder / could have been brought up badly by parents / could be amoral / could be an adrenalin junkie / could be from a poor background and was so hungry and tired that she had to break in / could be crying for attention from her parents, etc.

- Pupils could have a go at rewriting the story from Goldilocks' point of view.
or
Mediation: In groups pupils could role-play a mediation meeting between the bears, a mediator and Goldilocks. This should bring out their different interpretations.
or
Pupils could re-run the court case.

- Pupils could use role-play as a stimulus for thinking about different interpretations. One team can improvise a scene such as those in the following examples.
1 David was in trouble. He had hit Dean hard across the face, breaking his glasses. David was told to wait outside the office of his head of year while she called home. . . .
2 Sarah was caught shoplifting. Her parents were called to the store . . .
3 A paralysed man began to walk again after 30 years . . .

Groups should come up one at a time and improvise the situation that led up to the dramatised scene. The other groups should then have two to three minutes of thinking and discussing time before improvisation.

Learning objectives and outcomes

To understand and identify where selective information is being used in arguments.

To give alternative explanations for events.

Synopsis

B11: Looks at the 'selective information' argument.

There are many persuasive arguments about. However, are they giving us the whole picture?

B12: Looks at alternative perspectives. Goldilocks is being taken to court by the three bears . . . but is this a one-sided story?

Religious literacy: Words to be introduced – bias, interpretation, empathy.

Prior learning: None necessary. However, it is best studied in the context of argument evaluation.

Links: Drama, English, media studies, citizenship, business ethics, ethics, mediation. This topic also has links with argument building and seeing issues from all angles (see *Truth-Seekers: Thinking about God*, **B8 Rose-coloured glasses** and **B10 It's a miracle!**).

Background: We are bombarded with arguments from the media. Many arguments are of a poor quality and many are selective about the information they give us. Pupils also often lack skills of empathy in the playground or in class.

Pupils working at higher levels

B11 Half the story
- Who does the Greaser's crisps advert appeal to? How does it try to persuade? What hidden statements are in this advert?
(Greaser's cares about your health. Greaser's helps with community spirit. To be healthy you need to be fit.)

- Pupils to consider to what extent do businesses have a duty to be truthful in their advertising?

B12 Goldilocks behind bars
- Pupils could have a court case between different sets of characters from nursery rhymes or fairy tales, e.g. Jack vs Jill; the bad wolf vs Little Red Riding Hood; Cinderella vs her stepmother.

(A model for a court case can be found in *Truth-Seekers: Thinking about God's Nature*, **B19**)

- Pupils could take the morning newspaper and highlight any comments that appear biased and explain the bias.
Editorials are often a good place to start for this! It is interesting to provide articles on the same theme reported by different newspapers.

- Pupils could use de Bono's thinking hats (Yellow, Black, White) on a range of religious or ethical topics, in order to facilitate looking at a topic from different angles (see p. 5).

- Pupils could do some work on mediation, or begin a school mediation programme. See www. peaceworks.org.uk or www.nvc-resolutions.co.uk/peermediation.htm for examples.

Pupils working at lower levels

B11 Half the story
- Some pupils may find it easier to complete **B12 Goldilocks behind bars** before this page.
Pupils may need direct prompting questions to help them access the concepts, e.g. what is the flipside/hidden information?

B12 Goldilocks behind bars
- Flipside activity. Pupils can be given quick scenarios and asked to explain what the flipside (hidden consequences) of the scenario is. For example e.g. You win £5 million! (You might give up your job and be at a loose end. You might lose friends . . . or gain extra ones.)

- Pupils could role-play scenarios or adverts where clearly only one side of the picture is being shown. This could be extended to religious themes.

- Teachers may like to photocopy a picture that has a clear action scene, e.g. from a newspaper. The pupils can try to guess what has happened. After some discussion in which pupils give reasons for their ideas, the teacher should tell them what has happened as factually as possible.

Pupils could then stick speech or thought bubbles on the picture above each of the people. For each speech or thought bubble they should try to write a sentence or two about:
(a) How the person is feeling.
(b) What has happened from their point of view?

Teacher's notes: 4. How can we tell if something is being argued logically?

Suggested teaching activities

B13 Syllogisms

- Pupils are introduced to a syllogism – a logical argument with two premises and a following conclusion.

Valid arguments

- Pupils should read through the example and the explanation. It is worthwhile doing a few examples on the board in a whole class situation, or as small groups.

Pupils should then construct their own valid arguments and get a partner to check their work. It is useful for pupils to follow the frame of the first example when doing their own syllogisms (All . . . are . . .'). It is also helpful for them to initially write next to the argument how it works. Again, they can follow the pattern of the explanation given to the right of the example.

- Pupils should then invent some false valid arguments. Encourage them to be as silly as they like in doing this. They should be able to explain how each argument is valid. Example (b) is not a true (or sound) argument, as not all boys like football. (Note that C stands for conclusion and P1 and P2 stand for premise 1 and premise 2 respectively.)

- Pupils should have some practice at writing sound arguments.

- Finally pupils should look at the examples of invalid arguments. These are perhaps the hardest to recognise or generate for beginners. When making invalid arguments, pupils should look carefully at the second premise and work out if there is any other explanation for the conclusion. In the example about Kinna, it is certainly the case that Kinna could be a human. However, it is not a certainty. Kinna could be any animal that has blood.

- Pupils who are interested in practising syllogisms could play a syllogism builder game, in groups of three, using a spinner. (A spinner can be made by drawing a hexagon on card and dividing it into six segments. A pencil can be pushed through the middle – see **B13 ext Spinner template**.) Pupils build syllogisms, practising their understanding of true, false, valid and invalid syllogisms. They will need to create their own examples. The spinner should be half coloured red and half coloured green. Red sections stand for 'false' and green sections stand for 'true'. On alternate sections write the words 'valid' and 'invalid'. Number the players 1, 2 and 3.

Player 1 should spin the spinner without showing the others where it lands. If it lands on 'green', player 1 needs to write a first premise (premise 1) that is true (e.g. 'All humans are mammals'). If it lands on red, player 1 should write a false first premise (e.g. 'All humans are bananas').

Player 2 should then spin the spinner without showing the others where it lands. Player 2 should write premise 2 according to the colour of the spinner (true or false), and according to whether the spinner has landed on 'valid' or 'invalid' (e.g. A false invalid premise following a true premise 1 could be 'Fish are mammals'. A false valid premise might be 'Fish are humans'. An example of a true invalid premise is 'Cats are humans', and a true valid premise might be 'Your teacher is a human').

Player 3 should write the conclusion.

The group should analyse the final syllogism and explain whether it is a sound argument (giving reasons explaining why or why not).

The game should be played at least three times with each person being a different number each time.

Learning objectives and outcomes

To identify valid and invalid arguments with both true and false premises and conclusions.

To understand what a syllogism is and how to write syllogisms.

Synopsis

B13: Looks at analysing the validity of arguments.

Deductive reasoning is reasoning that is based on logic and not inferred from evidence.

Many religious and non-religious people put forward arguments to defend their position. However, are these arguments always sound?

Most arguments for God's existence rely on inductive reasoning. However, one famous argument – the ontological argument – is a deductive argument. This argument is challenging, even for many sixth-formers.)

Religious literacy: Words to be introduced – argument, flaw, valid, true, sound, syllogism, premise, conclusion.

Words that could be introduced at higher levels – deductive reasoning, logic.

Prior learning: None necessary.

Links: Maths.

Pupils working at higher levels

- Pupils could look up articles in newspapers and write syllogisms based on the article's main argument. They should highlight whether it is valid, invalid or sound.

- Pupils could research religious arguments that are based on testimonies. Are the arguments sound or not? This could be done through questioning people on why they believe in God, brainstorming, or researching traditional and modern arguments.

- To see whether pupils have logically consistent views about religion and God they could play the online game 'Battleground God' (*The Philosophers' Magazine*) at www.philosophersnet.com/games/god.htm

- Pupils could play around with syllogisms, turning valid arguments into invalid arguments, altering arguments to make them sound, etc. They could devise tests for each other.

Pupils working at lower levels

Some pupils may need some prompting questions to structure their answers. It might help for student to be given only the two premises and then make a conclusion themselves. Then they can compare their conclusion with the one on the sheet.

Pupils could then think of *all*/the ways that the conclusion could be reached.

- Pupils could progress to the Venn diagram pages to help them see whether premises are connected or not.

- There is also a differentiated sheet to aid understanding, **B14 Drawing the right conclusion.** Pupils are presented with six arguments, each with two or more conclusions. Pupils must underline the correct conclusion. Then pupils have to match up the muddled halves of definitions on the page.

- Finally, pupils have to work out which is the invalid argument and which is the valid argument. They could work in pairs and try to explain to their partner aloud why they are correct.

Background: A syllogism (also known as a categorical syllogism) is an argument with two premises and a conclusion. A famous example is: All men are mortal; Socrates is a man; therefore Socrates is mortal. A valid syllogism is one where the conclusion follows logically from its premises. However, it is important that we distinguish a valid argument from a true argument. Just because the syllogism is logically valid does not mean that it is necessarily true. A valid argument may have false premises or indeed a false conclusion and still be valid. When a syllogism is both valid and true, we call this a sound argument. Practice at analysing syllogisms should help to extend pupils' logical thinking skills. Practice should also enable pupils to highlight and critically examine weak arguments. With these benefits in mind, caution should be taken so that pupils realise that even if an argument is invalid or the premises are false, this does not mean that the conclusion could not be proved true through different premises. Likewise it is important that one flawed argument should not be portrayed as representing a set of beliefs.

Teacher's notes: 5. How can Venn diagrams help us to work out whether a syllogism is sound?

Suggested teaching activities

B15 Mr Venn's diagrams and B16 Venn-solved syllogisms

- Pupils need to be familiar with using Venn diagrams before proceeding to use them to illustrate syllogisms. The introduction (B15) could be skipped if pupils are confident in their use. The questions could be answered as a whole-class activity but pupils will benefit from practising alone.

- To extend creative thinking, pupils could randomly be given two or more pictures (of common objects) and asked to make a Venn diagram of the similarities.

- Once pupils are confident in using Venn diagrams they can proceed to using them as a visual aid for testing the validity of syllogisms. Pupils should make their way through the teaching examples on sheet B16. 3(c) might catch some pupils out.

The answer to question 2 is: invalid. Paul might be another denomination of Christianity. The answers to question 3 are: (a) invalid, but could have a true conclusion; (b) valid, needs more information; (c) valid and false; (d) invalid, true conclusion, not sound.

B17 Indirect syllogisms

A cheat's way of telling an invalid argument
By looking at the words one can quickly tell if an indirect argument is valid. If the same word is at the end of P1 and P2, then it is not a valid argument. However, be cautious when giving this information to pupils, as they will examine the word order and not work out the logic of the argument for themselves.

P1: All rats are vermin.
P2: Carrot is not vermin.
C: Carrot is not a rat.

The answers to sheet B16 are:
1 Tom is outside the circle as he cannot be a philosopher as philosophers like carrot cake and he does not. It is not sound as (to my knowledge) a prerequisite of good philosophising is not carrot cake eating.
2 (a) Alice is not over 18.
    (b) Dean is not a Muslim.
3 (a) No.
    (b) No.
    (c) Yes.

Learning objectives and outcomes

To understand how a Venn diagram can be used to visually solve syllogisms.

Synopsis

B15: Introduces Venn diagrams.

B16: Uses Venn diagrams to solve syllogisms.

B17: Pupils visually discover the validity of syllogisms through Venn diagrams.

Religious literacy: Words to be introduced – Venn diagram, classifying, logic, premise, conclusion, syllogism.

Prior learning: It is helpful if pupils have drawn Venn diagrams before, but not necessary. To understand the terminology of the page, it is important that pupils have covered syllogisms.

Links: Mathematics, logic.

Background: A Venn diagram is simply a field within which enclosed areas represent groups of items sharing common properties. It was invented by John Venn, who is famous exclusively for his diagrams. Venn diagrams are an extremely useful tool for teaching elements of logic. In this case they make syllogisms very clear for the visual learner. For information on syllogisms see Background on p. 36.

Pupils working at lower levels

- Pupils should spend time on finding common aspects between things to build their confidence in this area. Depending on their ability level, pupils could be asked to list common features between two:
  - fictional characters.
  - places of worship.
  - attitudes (in an article).
  - sets of numbers.

The more concrete the sets are, the easier this activity will be. To make this increasingly difficult, pupils could be given three or more sets.

- Some pupils may need to be explicitly guided through the process of making a Venn diagram. The main circle should refer to the main clause (the last word/s) of the first premise.

Example 3 (a) (sheet B16) should see mammals as the first circle drawn. An inner circle should represent cats, as cats are contained in the bigger category of mammals. It is not clear whether Clarence is a cat or another mammal. Therefore he should be in a separate circle with a question mark. This circle is inside the mammals circle but outside the cat circle.

- To help pupils formulate their own syllogisms they might need some practice at identifying and creating hierarchies. This is also good practice for mind maps. Either give pupils groups of words to arrange in a triangular hierarchy diagram, or give them a word or phrase (such as 'weather' or 'religion' or places of worship') and let them make their own.

Pupils working at higher levels

- For practice with Venn diagrams, pupils could be given two or more abstract images, or words, and asked to make a Venn diagram that illustrates the common and distinct features. These could be written on card and drawn at random out of a hat. This is a creative thinking exercise.

Teacher's notes: 5. How can Venn diagrams help us to work out whether a syllogism is sound?

Suggested teaching activities

B18 Flawed arguments

- Pupils are to read through the sheet and work out how each argument is flawed. The answers are below:

1 This is a poor argument. By its logic we would accept almost anything at all, including unicorns, the Easter bunny or flower fairies. There is a difference between having no reason to believe something and not having conclusive evidence. In the case of the Big Bang theory, scientists have solid grounds for believing it to be the case, even if direct proof has not been established.

2 This is not a valid argument. Just because we cannot see something does not mean that it does not exist. It is possible that there are other universes. The fact that we lack knowledge to confirm or reject this does not change facts about their existence. The argument also leads us to believe that a comparison between God and the tooth fairy is valid. This is a mistake as there is no evidence whatsoever for her/his real existence. This should be compared with the testimonies and revelation that support a belief in God. Even if we reject such evidence, the two cases are very different.

- Pupils could write syllogisms where the two things being compared are not truly comparable.

3 This argument is making a false assumption in premise 2. Premise 1 rightly states that either we were created or we were not created. However, the underlying assumption in P2 is that creation is a prerequisite of existence. If P2 is not true in itself then the whole argument fails. The cosmological argument makes a similar claim to P2 when it argues that there must be a first cause. This is an assumption that has been challenged.

- Pupils could write as many arguments as they can whereby the second premise is assumed but not proven.

4 This argument is flawed as it shows us only part of the picture. Reshma may indeed have seen God at the temple. We can also believe that Reshma, being an honest girl, did not lie. However, there may have been other grounds for Reshma believing that she saw God; she may have a neurological condition that gives her hallucinations; she may have dreamt the episode; she could have interpreted something incorrectly as God (such as a bright light or a loud noise, or tremor); she might have been on drugs; and so on.

- Pupils could think up as many reasons as they can to explain Reshma's vision. However, do explain that just because this argument is logically flawed does not mean that the original interpretation could not have been the correct one.

5 This argument is making the false expert mistake. Einstein had considerable expertise in physics. However, this does not mean that every belief of Einstein should be taken as correct, if it is outside his expert area.

- If pupils are struggling with this, the argument can be changed to give an example of a brilliant-minded atheist. Or to make the point clearer, what about some brilliant-minded people who have a more relaxed moral code? (See **B9 Evaluating arguments**.)

6 This is a similar argument to the one above. Just because Miss Take gets things wrong most of the time, it does not mean that she will get things wrong this time.

Learning objectives and outcomes

To identify flawed and weak logic in arguments, including false assumptions, weak arguments, valid and invalid arguments and selective information.

Synopsis

B18: Identifying arguments that are not sound. Religious people and non-religious people also use argument to back up what they are saying. Arguments can be persuasive. However, is it easy to tell which ones are sound?

Religious literacy: Words to be introduced – valid, invalid, true, false, sound, logic, premise, conclusion, syllogism.

Prior learning: Pupils should have covered all the material in this unit to be able to evaluate the different types of mistakes that are made in these arguments.

Links: This activity has links with the whole unit as it is a summary of some of the common problems found in arguments.

Background: See previous background information for more details. The arguments given on **B18** should be contrasted with true, valid arguments such as: *All children have to attend school until they are adults (age 16). Rakesh is a child (age 15). Therefore Rakesh has to attend school.*

Pupils working at higher levels

- Pupils could either make a poster to advertise a product (individually), or role-play an advert (in groups) in which they make a flawed or false argument. The class needs to guess what the flaw in the argument is.

Pupils working at lower levels

This activity is difficult and is recommended only for older or higher level pupils.

Teacher's notes: 6. Do we really know the essence of things?

Suggested teaching activities

B19 Defining moments

- Pupils to read sheet B18. Teachers may wish to show the passage on an interactive whiteboard, revealing each paragraph separately. Between sections, teachers could ask pupils to predict what the Zarg thinks the object will be.

- Pupils should have a go at defining other things. The more concrete they are the easier they will be, e.g. prayer, Mosque, holy books. Then move on to terms such as congregation, pilgrimage, God, etc.

B20 Socrates' challenge

- Pupils should be in twos or fours (in teams of two). They should throw the dice to decide who will be Socrates and who will be Glaucon. The team with the higher dice number should be Socrates, the other team, Glaucon. *Glaucon is in dialogue with Socrates in Plato's Republic. Glaucon invariably gives a poor definition of a thing which Socrates is keen to question.*

Socrates then throws the dice to determine what column they are to take the subject matter from. Glaucon throws to determine the row. This will give a word to define.

Glaucon's team starts by trying to define the object in question. They gain a point by doing so. Socrates can earn points by rejecting the definition while giving an example of how that definition could be used for another item also. A point should be removed if the teams repeat themselves.

The round ends when one of the teams can no longer give an example or definition. A second round should be played with Glaucon and Socrates swapping roles. If more than two rounds are to be played (in either the same, or successive lessons) then pupils can use the word grid like a game of Bingo. When they have won a row grid to reflect that word. The first team to get a row wins the game.

- Once pupils have the hang of defining concrete things, they could move on to more abstract concepts (see activity in column 3). Pupils could examine the essence of being human; goodness; existence. The resulting definitions could be expressed as poetry, abstract art or drama.

- Pupils to discuss whether creative expression captures the essence of a thing better than words. Pupils could discuss the famous quote 'a picture is worth a thousand words'.

B21 Summary

- The two boxes offer summary notes. The first is an A5-size summary of Arguing that may be helpful revision for some pupils. It can be copied and stuck in an exercise book. There is also a list of key words for the unit. The list is not comprehensive and pupils can add to it.

Learning objectives and outcomes

To attempt defining objects.

To recognise the difficulties in providing accurate definitions.

Synopsis

B19: The difficulties of defining objects.

The Zarg were having difficulty recognising things around them. This was largely due to inadequate definitions.

B20: A game providing practice in formulating accurate and comprehensive definitions.

Pupils are challenged to define objects as a starter exercise for learning Socratic Dialogue.

Religious literacy: Words to be introduced – Socratic dialogue, defining, abstract, concrete, essence.

Prior learning: None necessary.

Links: English language, debating.

Pupils working at higher levels

- Pupils can make a list of their own RE words to define (perhaps key words used in the last half term).

- Pupils should try to define more abstract concepts, such as knowledge, love, justice, truth, determination, etc.

- Pupils to think about whether, or why, it is important that we understand the true essence of the above.

- A 'challenge Socrates' competition could be set up where each week a word is to be defined as accurately as possible.

More able pupils could take it in turn to be Socrates and judge these definitions.

B20 Socrates' challenge

Teachers might like to limit the rows or columns that pupils should use, e.g. pupils could be restricted to selecting words from rows five and six, which are significantly harder. Alternatively, teachers or pupils may make their own grid to reflect ability, interest or cross-curricular themes, e.g. if pupils are studying *Romeo and Juliet* in English there could be appropriate connecting words such as love, hate, duty, family, tragedy, infatuation, law, fate, grudge.

Pupils working at lower levels

B20 Socrates' challenge

- Teachers might like to limit the rows or columns that certain pupils should use. The first three rows are probably the easiest.

Background: Socratic dialogue was the method of teaching favoured by Socrates and Plato. A good and accessible example of this can be found throughout Plato's *Republic*. Rather than imparting knowledge, the teacher asks the pupils a series of questions. Through the answering of additional questions, the field of thought is narrowed and the pupil comes to gain the required understanding or knowledge. Pupils are stretched to be as accurate as they can. This is a good exercise for developing critical thinking.

For more information on Socratic style question go to http://changingminds.org/techniques/questioning/socratic_questions.htm

B1 Building arguments (continued)

The bricks that we will use in argument building are:

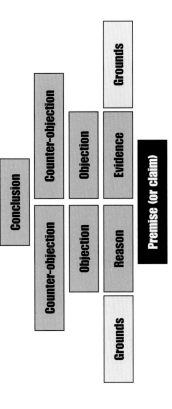

When building an argument our first brick is the claim we wish to make. This is the initial statement or premise. If this claim is to be a sound argument then we need to support it with other blocks. The blocks that will support the claim are our reasons.

• Write the statement 'God exists' in the centre of your page. Add at least two connecting reasons (use different reasons from the ones below).

❶

We need to anticipate the weaknesses in the argument. For this we need to consider objections to our reasons. An objection to the reason is useful as a test to see how strong the reason is.

❷

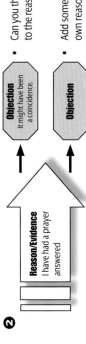

• Can you think of another objection to the reason on the left?

• Add some objections to your own reasons.

B1 continues

B1 Building arguments

A good bricklayer wants a strong wall. He knows where he should put different bricks. He knows his wall needs a solid structure. He anticipates the weaknesses in his wall before it is made. Building a good argument is a bit like building a wall. A good argument builder wants a strong argument. She knows where she should put her claims. She knows her argument will need a solid structure. She anticipates the weaknesses in her argument before the argument is made.

Wall building

Materials

Bricks: A wall is made up of different bricks. Each brick is important. The main bricks are rectangular, but they can be different sizes and shapes too.

Cement: This is essential for ensuring the bricks are connected to each other. Cement is a mixture of limestone, sand and water.

Tools

Spirit level: This is essential to know if a wall leans to one side. It is a ruler with a capsule of liquid in the middle.

Trowel: This is essential to make the wall tight. The wall will also look smooth and neat.

Considerations

Structure: The bricklayer must place bricks in a logical order to maintain strength.

Look: A builder must look at a wall from all angles.

Anticipate: Potential problems must be identified. These are often weak bricks or links.

Location: Where is the best place to put the wall?

Surveyor: A surveyor checks the wall to ensure that it is structurally sound.

Argument building

Materials

Bricks: An argument is made up of different parts. Each part is important. The main brick is the claim or premise. But reasons and evidence are also important. For strength there are objections, counter-objections and conclusions.

Cement: This is essential for ensuring arguments are connected to each other. Connecting words include *however* and *on the other hand*.

Tools

Spirit level: This is essential so we know if an argument leans to one side. We have to weigh up arguments carefully.

Trowel: Redrafting premises and conclusions is essential to make the argument tight. The argument will also look slick.

Considerations

Structure: An argument builder must place statements in a logical order to maintain strength.

Look: An argument builder must look at an argument from all angles.

Anticipate: Potential problems must be identified. These are often weak reasons or connections.

Location: Where is the best place to put the argument?

Surveyor: Get someone to survey your argument to ensure that it is structurally sound!

B1 continues

Truth-Seekers: **Thinking about Truth**

B2 Argument builder

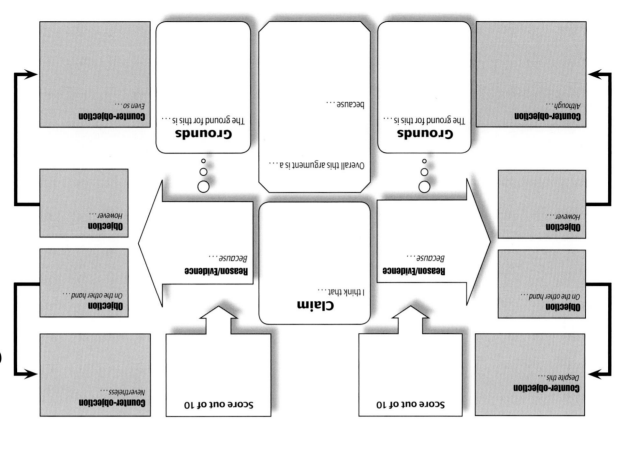

Truth-Seekers: **Thinking about Truth**

B1 Building arguments (continued)

Now we need to see if these objections are strong enough to withstand weight. An objection to an objection is called a counter-objection. If you can find a strong counter-objection then this strengthens your argument.

However, if you cannot find a strong counter-objection, then the objection will be stronger than your initial reason or evidence for the claim. If this is the case, you will not have a strong argument.

❸

> **Objection**
> It might have been a coincidence.
>
> ↑
>
> **Counter-objection**
> Just because something appears to be a coincidence does not mean that it is a coincidence.

- Can you think of another counter-objection to the objection on the left?
- Add some counter-objections to your own objections.
- Can you add any objections to your counter-objections?

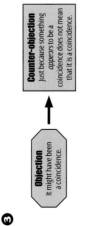

To connect all the parts of our argument together, we need to add some cement. Argument-building cement is connecting words and phrases.

- Go through your diagram and add connecting words and phrases above the arrows.

❹ Before we evaluate our argument, we must survey it properly and redraft parts if necessary.

- Does your argument make sense? Is it logical?
- Look at your argument from all possible angles.
- Does your argument lean to one side?
- Are you happy for your argument to lean to one side?
- If necessary redraft premises or conclusions.

Surveying arguments

It is now time to survey your argument. You need to evaluate it to see if it is a strong argument or not. Look again at your reasons:

Evidence/Reason	God exists	Reason/Evidence
Millions of people believe in God		I have had a prayer answered

We can work out how strong the reasons are if we look at what grounds those reasons. This means we have to look at what has caused our reasons.

B4 Arguing frames

Pie frame

Centre circle:
Title

2nd circle from the centre:
The statement or argument.

3rd circle from centre:
An explanation of the statement's arguments.

4th circle from centre:
This can be used for either examples or objections.

The middle line is accentuated so that students may use this as a for/against template.

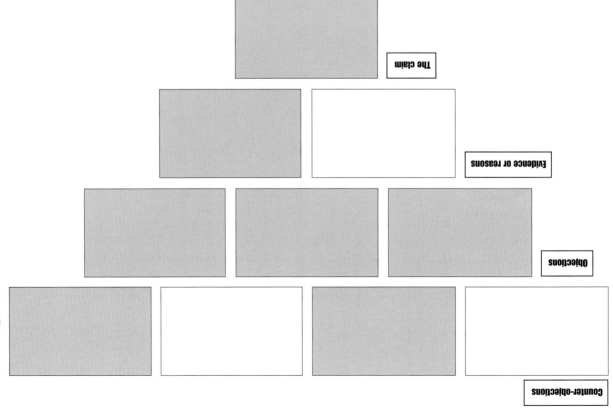

Evaluation planning frame

Introduction:

On the other hand . . .

The points I agree with:
Other   say that

The point of view that I disagree with:
Some   say that

My own opinion:
I agree with this because

Also

Another two points I disagree with:
1
2

Conclusion:
Therefore

B3 Argument wall

The claim

Evidence or reasons

Objections

Counter-objections

B6   Grounding reasons

Our reasons may be based on strong or weak evidence. There are seven main things that our reasons can be grounded on:

Personal testimony	Testimony of others	Expert opinion	Common knowledge	Empirical knowledge	Logic (or analytic)
This is when your own personal experience has led you to believe something is the case. For example, if you saw who kicked Sam yesterday at break, this is a personal testimony. It is not knowledge that is gained through others.	This is when others' experience has led you to believe that something is the case. For example, Anne told Sabah that she saw a ghost. Sabah has always trusted Anne and therefore believes her testimony.	This is a testimony from someone who can be trusted to give an accurate and knowledgeable opinion about something. An expert opinion needs the expert to: (a) Have real expertise in that area. (b) Be trustworthy in nature. (c) Have no conflict of interests.	This is knowledge that is generally accepted by all. For example, it is common knowledge that officially Christmas Day is celebrated on 25 December in the UK.	This is knowledge that has been tested in a scientific way. Our senses are essential in gaining empirical knowledge. For example, we know water boils at 100 degrees Celcius by heating water and watching the thermometer levels when it boils.	This is knowledge that is true by its own nature. It cannot be mistaken or wrong. Mathematical knowledge is logical knowledge. Other examples are statements that contain the conclusion in their definition, e.g. All mammals have warm blood.

Credibility Finally, we can ground our reason in assessing how reasonable or credible the premise (claim) is. Of course, this is very difficult to do, especially if we are not experts ourselves, or if we have no experience of it.

- Look at your reasons. In each case state what grounds your reason.
- Look at all the grounds for reasons. Rearrange them so that the strongest ground is at the top and the weakest ground is at the bottom. Give your reasons for your choices.
- What are the grounds for your objections and counter-objections?
- Look at the table below. Find examples of strong and weak grounds of knowledge and fill them in.

Ground of knowledge	Examples – Strong	Examples – Weak
Personal testimony		
Testimony of others		
Expert opinion		
Common knowledge		
Empirical knowledge		
Logic	Logic, by its nature, will always be strong.	

- Now you know what grounds your reasons, you can evaluate them.
- Give each reason a score out of 10 for strength.

B5   Big points and little points

When you are arguing a case, each main point you make should have supporting evidence. These help to make your case stronger.

Instructions

The cards below all give a view on the question 'Does God exist?'

1. Cut out the separate cards (if it is not already done).
2. Separate the cards into two piles: cards that support the view that God exists and cards that do not support the view that God exists. You should have 10 cards in each pile.
3. Each pile will contain two main points. Each main (big) point will have four (little) pieces of supporting evidence.
4. Place the cards with supporting evidence underneath the main cards in order of argument strength.
5. Shade the strongest point for and against the question.
6. Use these cards to form an essay answering the question 'Does God exist?'

Many people from different religions have experienced God.	'The world is saturated with beauty at a microscopic and macroscopic level. The world must have been designed that way.' (F R Tennant)	A good God would never allow evil and suffering to occur.	We have no concrete proof that God exists.
In Fatima, Mary appeared to three small children. Mary gave them messages which they claimed came true.	There is evidence of good design in the world. Look at a banana: It is nutritious, tasty, and comes sealed and protected in an easily peelable skin.	Millions of innocent people have been injured or killed in wars around the world.	Many religious people pray to God and never get their prayers answered.
Muhammed (pbuh) was told the Qur'an by an angel sent from God.	If we found a watch on the ground we would assume someone created it. The world is far more complex than a watch!	Children and babies who have done nothing wrong die too.	The human body may look as if it is intelligently designed, but we could have evolved that way without a creator.
Many people have experienced the feeling that there is a presence bigger than themselves, or a feeling of awe and wonder.	Human designs and inventions have mirrored the natural world in many ways. We have copied birds flying by creating aeroplanes.	There are many natural disasters for which humans are not responsible. Volcanoes and earthquakes cause great suffering.	The world does not need a creator. It could have existed for all eternity.
Miracles occur in many religions each year. At Lourdes in France people gather every day to pray and be cured of sickness.	The human body is symmetrical. Symmetry and pattern is found throughout nature. Just take flowers, for instance!	There are many diseases and illnesses that cause great pain. A perfect God would not create bodies that went wrong.	Plants and animals that look like they are well designed could have evolved that way.

B8 Reasons for reasons

Have you ever wondered what reasons you have for having your reasons? All our reasons are based on something else. Below are some of the things that our reasons are based (grounded) on:

Personal testimony	Testimony of others	Expert opinion	Common knowledge	Empirical knowledge	Logic (or analytic)	Credibility

- Look at the quotes below. What are the grounds for their reasons?
- Are the reasons good reasons or not? Rate each reason out of 10.

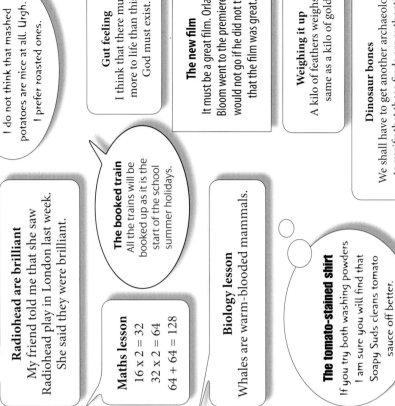

Potatoes

I do not think that mashed potatoes are nice at all. Urgh. I prefer roasted ones.

Gut feeling

I think that there must be more to life than this, so God must exist.

The new film

It must be a great film. Orlando Bloom went to the premiere. He would not go if he did not think that the film was great.

Weighing it up

A kilo of feathers weighs the same as a kilo of gold.

Dinosaur bones

We shall have to get another archaeologist to verify that these finds are authentic.

Radiohead are brilliant

My friend told me that she saw Radiohead play in London last week. She said they were brilliant.

The booked train

All the trains will be booked up as it is the start of the school summer holidays.

Maths lesson

16 x 2 = 32
32 x 2 = 64
64 + 64 = 128

Biology lesson

Whales are warm-blooded mammals.

The tomato-stained shirt

If you try both washing powders I am sure you will find that Soapy Suds cleans tomato sauce off better.

B7 Evaluation scale

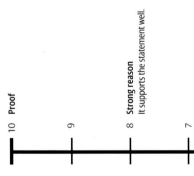

10 **Proof**

9

8 **Strong reason**
It supports the statement well.

7

6

5 **Fair reason**
It supports the statement to some extent.

4

3

2 **Very weak reason**
This does not support the statement very well.

1

0 **No reason**

B10 Whose opinion should I trust?

The experts below are promoting some products at the Advertisers' Expert lunch. They have agreed to lend their support as in their expert opinion they think that the products are really good. However, during the course of the lunch their notes have been muddled up.

Look at the claims made below.

- Whose opinion would you trust? Why?
- Whose opinion would you not trust? Why?
- Can you get the right notes back to the right expert?

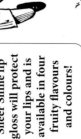

Sheer Shine lip gloss will protect your lips and is available in four fruity flavours and colours!

Grippers give me the stability I need even in mud!

Foamy Stubble™ shaving cream gives the closest shave ever!

I recommend using InternetClear communications for all your business needs.

Woof! Woof!

For this recipe use Choco-o-Chocolate. With 70% cocoa solids it gives a richer taste.

Bingo's Crunchy Dog Chews give dogs all the nutrition they need and a glossy coat!

For the best classical music go to the Concerto website.

B9   Evaluating arguments

Philosophers always use arguments to make a point. This is not to say that philosophers are angry people, or that they enjoy fights. To put forward an argument is to put forward and justify a particular point of view.

The false expert

Arguments are used everywhere. You might not even be aware of them.

In Spring 2008 Barack Obama was in full swing trying to persuade people to choose him as a candidate for the next presidential election in the USA. He gathered together a wide range of supporters who publically endorsed his campaign. These included a television talk show host (Oprah Winfrey) and a range of movie actors (Robert de Niro, Tom Hanks, Scarlett Johansson and Halle Berry).

- Are these people experts on the issues that are important in electing a leader of a country?
- What are these people experts in?
- Are you more or less likely to support a politician if a famous person supports them? Why?

Sneekers' Shoes are making an argument. They are arguing that their RunMax trainers are the ultimate shoes. However, this is not a particularly good argument.

- Can you work out why?
- Would you be persuaded by Sneekers?
- What would persuade you to buy them?

To think about . . . .

When you are looking at claims that are supported by others then ask yourself three questions:

– Are they generally trustworthy in character?
– Are they a genuine expert in the area?
– Do they have conflicting interests?

Look at the quote below. It is from Mother Teresa. She was a nun, best known for selflessly helping the poor and sick in a poverty-stricken part of India.

- What is the argument she is making?
- If we regard Mother Teresa as an expert, what was her area of expertise?
- Is her claim a strong claim or not?

'Any country that accepts abortion, is not teaching its people to love, but to use any violence to get what it wants.'

Mother Teresa

B11 Half the story

Greaser's Crisps

help you and your family to stay fit!

Official Greaser Token

Collect Greaser's Crisps tokens.
For every 1000 tokens we
provide sports equipment
for YOUR
community.

Greaser's cares

- Look at the argument for buying Greaser's crisps.
- Why would someone want to buy Greaser's crisps?
- What is their main argument?
- Is this a good argument?

The above advert is making an argument. However, the argument is not a very good one. Unfortunately, this type of argument can be seen on billboards everywhere. The problem with this type of argument is that they are not showing us the whole picture. It is true that eating a huge amount of Greaser's crisps will help buy gym equipment. It is true that this would give us the means to exercise. However, this has to be balanced with eating copious amounts of Greaser's crisps. Crisps are high in salt and fat. A large quantity would certainly be bad for our health.

Look at this argument below. It certainly *seems* sound . . .

Fibre is good for our hearts.
Branuflakes contain fibre.
Branuflakes are good for our hearts.

Branuflakes Nutritional Information	
Bran	lots
Wheat	loads
Fibre	not much
Fruit	a little
Salt	way too much
Fat	50%
Sugar	High

- Look at these adverts.
- What is the argument in each case?
- What information are they leaving out?
- Are these arguments persuasive? Give reasons.

Save our foxes!
Ban the vile 'sport' of fox-hunting now!

A plea from our hearts — help save our children with diabetes!
Medical laboratory research is the only way. Donate your money by phone or email now!

However, it does not give us the whole picture. Branuflakes do contain fibre, but the nutritional card tells us more information.

- If you saw only the front of the box, what would be your impression of Branuflakes?
- What extra information does the nutritional card give us?
- Is the Branuflakes' argument true? Give your reasons why.

B12 Goldilocks behind bars

'Live from the High Court . . . the case of the three bears vs Goldilocks. We join them now as the prosecution team are making their case . . .'

Once upon a time there was an impertinent, destructive, nosy little girl called Goldilocks. She was up to no good, wandering in the woods (against the wish of her mother, no doubt). She came across a rather fine house. Jealousy overcame her and she wandered in. Isn't that right, Goldilocks? The trespasser! Now, in this house lived three noble bears. The first bear was a handsome big bear, the second a cuddly middle-sized bear and the third was a cute tiny little bear. The bears were out for their usual pre-brunch stroll. They had left their porridge to cool on the table in three bowls. The bears always made delightful porridge, and they were looking forward to it greatly. Goldilocks, as bold as brass, stole (yes, your Honour, stole!) from the first bowl. 'Ouch this is too hot,' she said in a later statement. She then tried the second bowl. 'Oohh, now that is too cold!' she said. Not content, she tried the tiny bowl, 'Mmmm, that is just right,' and then ate the porridge all up! Not one mouthful she left for poor Tiny Bear. Thieving is apparently tiring work, so tiring that she then sat down on the bear's priceless antique chairs. Well, well, the first chair was too hard. 'Oww!' she exclaimed. The second chair was apparently too soft for her liking also! The third chair that she tried she claimed was 'just right'. Goldilocks sat in the chair until it snapped under her heavy weight. Not content with her trail of damage and destruction, she ran upstairs. She saw three beds. She tried the first bed. 'Oh this is way too hard,' she said. Then she collapsed

into the middle bed. 'This is way too soft for me,' she said. She finally tried the third bed. 'Ahhhh, this is just right!'; carrying on as if it were her own home!

The three bears, hungry after their exercise, decided to come back for their porridge. They came back to a shock. Someone had been eating from their porridge bowls! Tiny Bear was shocked to find that someone had eaten his all up! Then they went to sit down. The bears found that somebody had been sitting in all their chairs. Tiny Bear sobbed, 'And they have broken my chair, the one that Dad made me for Christmas!' Finally the bears got suspicious, and with fear in their hearts, went upstairs to the bedroom. There they saw that someone had been sleeping in all their beds . . . and in Tiny Bear's bed there lay a sleeping girl! The nerve of it all! A GIRL of all things! With all her human germs and infections! Big Bear, in defence, roared at the top of his voice. (Very restrained I should say – if I was a bear I would have eaten HER up, your honour!) Goldilocks, not so bold now, ran as fast as her legs could carry her away from the house. The bears realised that this was not the golden age was passed and this was not the neighbourhood it used to be. They installed a home security device (the Big Bad Wolf) and got house insurance. Your honour, members of the jury, I say to you today that Goldilocks is guilty of a multitude of crimes: TRESPASS, DAMAGE TO PROPERTY AND ROBBERY! The bears need to be duly compensated. I hope today, that justice will be done.

'Well News @ 9 viewers, now comes the defence team . . . and they had better be good if Goldilocks is to stand a chance tonight!'

You are on the defence team for Goldilocks. Prepare a case on her behalf. Think about:

- What evidence of bias is there from the prosecution?
- Goldilocks did not have time to speak to Big Bear before she ran away. What might she have said?
- What might explain Goldilocks' actions on that morning?

B13 Syllogisms

Valid arguments

One type of argument is called a **syllogism**. A syllogism has two statements (called premises), and a conclusion that follows logically from the premises.

Premise 1: All humans have blood.
Premise 2: Kinna is a human.
Conclusion: Therefore Kinna has blood.

If it is the case that **all** humans have blood, and Kinna is a human, then logically she must have blood too.

• Using the model above, write your own syllogism.
  Get a partner to check that it is logical.

A logical argument is called a **valid** argument. An argument can be true or false and still be logical. Look at the examples below:

(a)
Premise 1: All cats are fish.
Premise 2: Cally is a cat.
Conclusion: Therefore Cally is a fish.

(b)
Premise 1: All boys like football.
Premise 2: Adam is a boy.
Conclusion: Therefore Adam likes football.

If it is the case that **all** cats are fish, and Cally is a cat, then logically she must be a fish. However, we know that it is not the case that all cats are fish. This argument works; it is valid, however it is also untrue. False argument.

• (b) is a valid argument. Explain whether it is also true or not

• Invent two syllogisms that are valid, yet untrue.

Sound arguments

A sound argument is one that is both valid and true.

• Are there any sound arguments on these pages?

• Invent a syllogism that is sound.

Invalid arguments

An invalid syllogism is one where the conclusion does not follow on logically from the premises. It is a flawed argument. Look at the argument below:

Premise 1: All humans have blood.
Premise 2: Kinna has blood.
Conclusion: Therefore Kinna is human.

This is an invalid argument. Even though Kinna has blood, and all humans have blood too, this does mean that she is human. Other animals have blood too. In this case, Kinna is a pet rabbit.

• Invent some invalid arguments. Are your arguments sound or not?

B14 Drawing the right conclusion

Look at the arguments below. Underline the correct conclusion.

1 *Premise 1: All humans have blood.*
Premise 2: Kinna is a human.
Conclusion: Therefore Kinna has blood.
Conclusion: Therefore Kinna might have blood.

2 *Premise 1: All humans have blood.*
Premise 2: Kinna has blood.
Conclusion: Therefore Kinna is a human.
Conclusion: Therefore Kinna might be a human.

3 *Premise 1: All boys like football.*
Premise 2: Adam likes football.
Conclusion: Adam is a boy.
Conclusion: Adam could be a boy.

4 *Premise 1: All boys like football.*
Premise 2: Adam is a boy.
Conclusion: Therefore Adam likes football.
Conclusion: Therefore Adam might like football.

5 *Premise 1: All cats are fish.*
Premise 2: Cally is a cat.
Conclusion: Cally is a fish.
Conclusion: Cally is a catfish.
Conclusion: Cally might be a fish.

6 *Premise 1: All cats are fish.*
Premise 2: Cally is a fish.
Conclusion: Cally is a cat.
Conclusion: Cally might be a cat.
Conclusion: Cally is a catfish.

Muddled definitions

Match up the correct halves of each argument.

A sound argument is… …one that is not logical.

A valid argument is… …one that is logical but false.

A invalid argument is… …one that is both logical and true.

A valid but unsound argument is… …one that is logical.

Look at the arguments opposite. One is sound and one is not. Which is which? Explain how you know.

Premise 1: All dancers move.
Premise 2: Mekell is a dancer.
Conclusion: Mekell moves.

Premise 1: All dancers move.
Premise 2: Mekell moves.
Conclusion: Mekell is a dancer.

B16 Venn-solved syllogisms

It can sometimes be hard to work out whether an argument is valid or sound. Some people find that it helps to try out the logic of an argument visually. One way of doing this is through a Venn diagram.

1 Look at the following argument. It is called a syllogism. This is an argument that has two statements (called premises) and a conclusion that logically follows from the premises.

> *Premise 1: All Catholics are Christians.*
> *Premise 2: Paul is a Catholic.*
> *Conclusion: Paul is a Christian.*

We can work out whether the argument is valid or not with a diagram. In our main circle we have the word 'Christians'. We know that all Catholics are Christians, so we place the word 'Catholics' within the Christian circle. We know that Paul is a Catholic so we place Paul within the 'Catholic' circle. We can see our conclusion very easily from the diagram – Paul is Christian as he is within the 'Christian' circle.

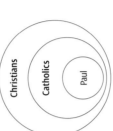

But is this a sound argument?

To see if this is a sound argument we need to ask Paul one thing. What is that thing? If it is a sound argument, what will be his reply?

A sound argument is both valid and true!

2 Now look at the following syllogism:

> *Premise 1: All Catholics are Christians.*
> *Premise 2: Paul is a Christian.*
> *Conclusion: Paul is a Catholic.*

- Look at the diagram above. Do you think that the conclusion is valid?

In the 'Christians' circle we can put Catholics as we are told in Premise 1 that all Catholics are Christians. We can also put Paul in the 'Christians' circle as premise 2 tells us that Paul is a Christian. However, we do not have enough information to say whether Paul is a Catholic or not. We cannot put him in the 'Catholics' circle as we do not know.

- Why might Paul not be a Catholic?

3 Make your own Venn diagrams to work out the validity of the following arguments:

a
> *Premise 1: All cats are mammals.*
> *Premise 2: Clarence is a mammal.*
> *Conclusion: Therefore Clarence is a cat.*

b
> *Premise 1: All Zarg are Theodotupuki.*
> *Premise 2: Zandis is a Zarg.*
> *Conclusion: Therefore Zandis is a Theodotupuki.*

c
> *Premise 1: All Tellytubbies eat toast.*
> *Premise 2: Po eats toast.*
> *Conclusion: Therefore Po is a Tellytubby.*

- Which syllogisms are invalid?
- Which syllogisms are valid?
- Which of these syllogisms has a true conclusion but is still invalid?
- Make up your own syllogisms. For each one draw a Venn diagram to illustrate its validity.

B15 Mr Venn's diagrams

A Venn diagram can help us compare two or more things, showing aspects they have in common in the overlapping section.

Look at the Venn diagram below. Islam and Christianity are different religions. However, they share many things in common. One thing they share in common is belief in one God.

- How many other things do Christianity and Islam have in common?

- Where should you put these things in the Venn diagram. Why?

John Venn was a mathematician who lived from 1834 to 1923. He is most famous for inventing the Venn diagram.

Islam   *Belief in one God*   **Christianity**

B18 Flawed arguments

Look at the arguments below. For each one work out how the argument is flawed. You might like to work them out using Venn diagrams.

1
- 4 billion people around the world believe in God, despite having no concrete proof.
- We haven't got complete proof for a number of things that are widely accepted by billions of people, such as the Big Bang or evolution.
- Therefore there is no problem in accepting that God exists.

2
- Adults do not believe in the tooth fairy as they have never seen her.
- We have never seen God.
- Therefore there is no reason to believe in God.

3
- Either we were created or we were not created.
- If we were not created then we wouldn't exist.
- We do exist.
- Therefore God must exist.

4
- Reshma said that she saw God at the temple.
- The lie detector test said that she was not lying.
- Therefore Reshma saw God.

5
- Einstein was one of the most brilliant minds ever!
- Einstein believed in God.
- Therefore, if you are brainy, you will believe in God too!

6
- Miss Take has a reputation for making mistakes and getting things wrong.
- Miss Take said that God exists.
- Therefore Miss Take has made a mistake this time and God must not exist.

B17 Indirect syllogisms

Syllogisms that have positive premises are called direct syllogisms. The premises of a direct syllogism talk about something happening or being the case. A valid direct syllogism will have a conclusion that speaks about something being the case. All the previous syllogisms have been direct syllogisms.

Some arguments have premises that are negative. Their premises talk of something not happening, or not being the case. These types of syllogisms are indirect syllogisms. A valid indirect syllogism will have a conclusion that also speaks of something not being the case. We can work out our Venn diagrams for indirect syllogisms in the same way as with direct syllogisms.

1 Look at the following example of a valid indirect syllogism.

- Why is Tom outside the main circle?

Premise 1: All philosophers eat carrot cake.
Premise 2: Tom does not eat carrot cake.
Conclusion: Therefore Tom is not a philosopher.

- Is this a sound argument? Why or why not?

2 Write the following conclusions and draw Venn diagrams to express the following arguments:

a *Premise 1:* Everybody who is 18 or over can vote.
Premise 2: Alice cannot vote.
Conclusion: Therefore . . . .

b *Premise 1:* All Muslims follow Islam.
Premise 2: Dean does not follow Islam.
Conclusion: Therefore . . . .

- Now make up three invalid syllogisms. Represent them in the form of Venn diagrams.

3 Draw a Venn diagram for each of the following arguments:

- Are any of these arguments sound?

a *Premise 1:* Saints are very holy people.
Premise 2: Bob is very holy.
Conclusion: Therefore Bob is a saint.

b *Premise 1:* Saints are very holy people.
Premise 2: Bob is not a saint.
Conclusion: Bob is not holy.

c *Premise 1:* Muslims pray five times a day.
Premise 2: Michael does not pray five times a day.
Conclusion: Michael is not a Muslim.

B20 Socrates' challenge

No dictionaries allowed!

	1	2	3	4	5
1	Bed	Lampshade	Desk	Book	Pen
2	The park	Skateboard	Swimming pool	Skirt	Table
3	Mouse	Knife	Candle	Tree	Glasses
4	Wardrobe	Llama	Car	Mountain	Adult
5	Dinner	Electricity	Playing	Fire	Games

Scenario

Glaucon and Socrates are having a discussion about the true meaning of things. Glaucon thinks he is very good at defining things, but Socrates is not so sure it is that easy. Can you meet Socrates' challenge?

Instructions

➤ Throw the dice. The team with the higher number will be Socrates, the team with the lower number will be Glaucon.

➤ To find out what you are defining:

Socrates must throw the dice to determine the column. A 6 means a free choice. Then Glaucon should throw to choose the row. Again, a 6 means a free choice.

Scoring

➤ Glaucon gets 1 point each time he narrows the definition down.

➤ Socrates gets 1 point for every time he rejects the definition *and* gives an example of how the given definition could be used for other things also.

➤ 1 point is deducted every time someone repeats themselves.

Judging

➤ The winning team is the one that makes a definition (Glaucon), or gives an example (Socrates) that the other team cannot respond to.

➤ There should be at least two rounds (two separate words to define). In the second round, Glaucon and Socrates should swap roles.

B19 Defining moments

Zandis, chief Zarg from the planet Zog, was having trouble adapting to the human way of life. Many objects were unfamiliar to him. Although he had learnt a lot during his stay on earth many practices still seemed rather odd.

He had spent many hours in libraries adding to his knowledge banks. The problem was that the knowledge he had gained did not seem to correspond with reality. For instance, he knew that a horse was a gramnivorous quadruped with 40 teeth. However, as he couldn't reach into an animal's mouth to count the teeth, he often could not distinguish a cow from a horse. He knew that a church was where people prayed, but he was having difficulty finding one. If he could not find a church then he could not observe the believers.

He carefully looked around the town. He thought to himself: It's Sunday and it's 10 a.m. People are well-dressed and hurrying inside this building. They have purses in their hands, ready to donate money. It must be a church service! I have found a church at last!

However, it was not a church. It was a department store. He went in search again. This time he saw a symbol of Christianity that he had read about on the front of the building: a cross. Again,

as he drew closer, he saw people sitting inside. They were quiet. Some of them looked worried. A church, definitely, he thought. The cross is clearly displayed on the front of the building. These people are concentrating on their prayers, or are sorry for their sins. I will go inside quietly.

As he made his way inside, a nurse stopped him at the door. 'Strictly no admittance unless you are a relative,' she said. It was clear that he had not found a church.

• In pairs, help Zandis define the following things accurately. Person A needs to provide a definition of the item or idea. Person B needs to see whether this is a good definition, or whether the definition could be used for something else as well. Continue until each item is defined properly.

Define the following: prayer, Mosque, holy books, God, congregation and pilgrimage.

Extension: *Try to define harder concepts, such as existence, love, justice, truth.*
What things are easier to define?
What are the hardest things to define and why?

B21 Summary

Key words

Argument – A case that is made for believing that something is true.

Premise – A statement that is assumed to be true, and from which conclusions are drawn.

Conclusion – A judgement we make after carefully considering evidence and reason.

Conclusion (of a logic argument) – A statement that must follow if we accept the premises.

Ground – What the premise of judgement is based on.

Claim – An assertion that something is the case, or is true.

Objection (of an argument) – Disagreeing with a reason.

Counter-objection – Disagreeing with that objection.

Rebuttal – An objection.

Empirical – Knowledge gained from experience and observation.

Personal testimony – An assertion by yourself based on first-hand experience.

Testimony of others – An assertion by others based on their experience.

Logic – Reasoning (that cannot be faulted).

Valid – A valid argument is an argument that works logically.

Sound – An argument that is both true and valid.

Arguing

Follow these steps when you are building an argument.

It will help you to consider all possibilities.

Follow these steps when you evaluate an argument:

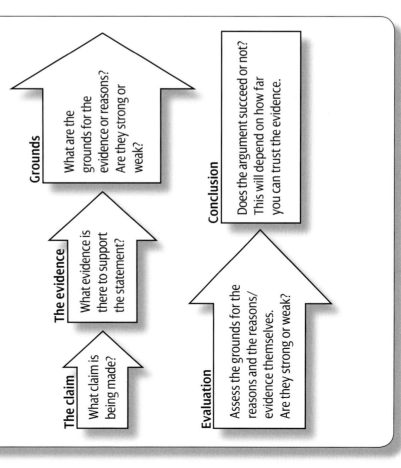

The claim
What claim is being made?

The evidence
What evidence is there to support the statement?

Grounds
What are the grounds for the evidence or reasons? Are they strong or weak?

Evaluation
Assess the grounds for the reasons and the reasons/evidence themselves. Are they strong or weak?

Conclusion
Does the argument succeed or not? This will depend on how far you can trust the evidence.

Unit C **What is truth?**

About the unit

This unit suggests activities and support material that can be used in teaching and learning about truth. There are three main learning areas split into five key questions. First, the unit makes an attempt to help pupils clarify and respond to the question, 'What is truth?' and consider whether truth claims are mutually exclusive. It aims to encourage thinking about the wider issues of proof, evidence, probability and certainty, in relation to belief. Second, the unit considers access to the truth, and whether it is possible to move nearer to/reach the truth. Finally, issues of truth, such as the importance of truth, or what we do with truth, are considered.

While it is proper to acknowledge that this unit has developed from a critical realist perspective, it does not assume that pupils and teachers also subscribe to this model of truth. Pupils are encouraged to explore different interpretations of truth, including both realist and relativist approaches, whether these are theistic or non-theistic. There is an emphasis in this unit on developing skills such as interpretation, evaluation and analysis, which enable pupils to reflect on their personal beliefs and articulate them coherently.

Where this unit fits in

This unit links with the following key stage 3 guidelines in the non-statutory national framework for RE:

- Learning about religion: 1a, 1d, 1f, 1g
- Learning from religion: 2a, 2b, 2e
- Religions and beliefs: 3a, 3b, 3d
- Themes: 3e, 3f, 3g
- Experiences and opportunities: 3o, 3p, 3q, 3r

This unit links with the following GCSE and AS/A level RS specifications:

GCSE specifications – AQA RS specification B, EdExcel (Religion and Life specification A), OCR (Religion and Philosophy specification B) and WJEC RS (B). AS and A Level specifications – EdExcel, OCR, AQA (Philosophy of Religion unit).

This unit would help to prepare pupils for later GCSE work in RS by developing their ability for independent critical thinking, and consideration of the concepts of proof and truth.

Attitudes in the unit

This unit helps pupils develop the following four attitudes outlined in the non-statutory national framework for RE:

Self awareness Becoming increasingly sensitive to the impact of their ideas and behaviour on other people, *e.g. understanding how the claim to truth impacts on others.*

Respect for all Being prepared to recognise and acknowledge their own bias, *e.g. when discussing matters of personal conviction.*

Open-mindedness Being willing to go beyond surface impressions, *e.g. in using questions in order to probe deeper.*

Appreciation and wonder Recognising that knowledge is bounded by mystery, *e.g. when reflecting on the verification of truth claims, or the nature of truth itself.*

Learning objectives and outcomes

Pupils will consider what it means to say something is true, giving an informed personal response. They will look at two main perspectives of truth (realism and post modernism), and what it might mean to talk about religious, moral and historical truths. When reflecting on the nature of religious truth claims, pupils will discuss the possibility of pluralism, and absolutism. They will understand how religious truth claims are different from, say, scientific ones. They will be able to use a wide religious and philosophical vocabulary. Pupils will use question-generation in seeking a deeper understanding of the truth. They will also look at issues concerning truth, such as defending the truth and the importance of truth.

At lower levels: pupils will be able to understand what we mean by the word 'truth' in general usage, and will be able to give a response to the question, 'Should we always tell the truth?' Pupils will understand that different perspectives will alter our perception of events, and this will make it difficult to assign truth in some circumstances. Pupils will be able to ask relevant questions.

At higher levels: pupils will have critiqued relativist and realist approaches to truth. They will be able to identify links between proof, faith and truth. They will have looked at issues surrounding truth, e.g. the Truth and Justice Commission in post-apartheid South Africa, and whether they agree with the principles behind it. They will be able to ask pertinent questions that can open up areas of further research/thought. They will have reflected on whether religious truth can be verified, and whether belief lies outside the boundaries of rationality.

Assessment example

(based on the task on p. 58) C4 What is truth like?

Pupils should select a picture from the worksheet and explain (a) what model of truth the picture tries to encapsulate, describing that model of truth; (b) how the symbolism relates to that model of truth. For levels 6, 7 and 8 pupils additionally (c) explain to what extent does the picture accurately represent truth. Pupils should complete this assessment only after they have looked at a range of approaches to the truth, including discussion of postmodernism and realism. This assessment allows pupils to show understanding between level 4 and level 8. The aim is to assess pupils' understanding of the different approaches to truth, their ability to reflect on a personal understanding of truth, and the strengths and weaknesses (at higher levels) of using symbols to explain concepts.

Level 4: Pupils working at level 4 will understand the terms absolutism and postmodernism. They should be able to describe one model of truth, select an appropriate picture from the page and explain how it relates to truth.

Level 5: Pupils working at level 5 will understand the terms absolutism, pluralism, realism and postmodernism. They should be able to select an appropriate picture from the page or choose their own example, describe it clearly and explain how the symbolism relates to truth. They will be able to use some specialist religious and philosophical vocabulary in explaining their answer.

Level 6: Pupils working at level 6 will understand the terms absolutism, pluralism, realism and postmodernism. They will select one model of truth and describe it accurately, with detail. They should be able to select an appropriate picture from the page, choose their own example/make up their own example and explain in detail how the symbolism relates to truth. In answering the question (c), they will make a reasoned judgement, referring to both sides of the argument. They will be able to use some specialist religious and philosophical vocabulary in explaining their answer, and words such as ambiguity, perspective, partial, belief.

Level 7: Pupils working at level 7 will understand terms such as absolutism, pluralism, realism, relativism and postmodernism. They will use a wide range of religious and philosophical vocabulary in discussing both sides of the argument in part (c), recognising both the strengths and the limitations of symbols to express concepts. They will show a coherent understanding and analysis of the model of truth that they have chosen. They should be able to select an appropriate picture from the page, choose/modify or make up their own example and explain in detail how the symbolism relates to truth.

Useful background resources

Teacher books: *Philosophers and Religious Truth* – Ninian Smart
An Interpretation of Religion – John Hick
What is Truth? – Peter Vardy
Truth: A Guide for the Perplexed – Simon Blackburn
Why Truth Matters – Jeremy Stangroom and Ophelia Benson

Films: *The Matrix* I and II;
The Truman Show

Links to world religions

While many religions are absolutist about their truth claims, a number of religions offer pluralist perspectives.

In Sikhism, the Guru Granth Sahib makes several pluralist claims. On pages 12 and 13 we read, 'The seconds, minutes, and hours, days, weeks and months and various seasons originate from the One Sun; O Nanak, in just the same way, the many forms originate from the Creator.' On page 1350 there is a direct reference to other religions: 'Do not say that the Vedas, the Bible and the Qur'an are false. Those who do not contemplate them are false.'

Hinduism teaches that there are many paths to the truth – none of which exclusively hold or encapsulate the truth. A hymn from the Rig Veda (1.164.46) states that 'Truth is One, but the sages call Him by many names.'

Religious literacy

Through the activities in this unit pupils will understand, use and spell correctly the following words and terms: *absolute, accurate, ambiguity, belief, clarity, conflict, depth, fact, lying, opinion, partial, perspective, pluralism, postmodernist, realist, reasoned judgement, relative, tolerance, truth, truth-claims, understanding.*

Index of key questions and related activity sheets

Note: **core activities are listed in bold**; *extension activities are listed in italic.*

Teacher's notes: 1. What is truth?

Suggested teaching activities

C1 Is there more than one type of truth?

- Pupils to think about what the word truth means. Pupils could try to articulate this in their books as a piece of formative assessment or orally. There should be class feedback.
- Pupils to read through the sheet. They could give an example of each type of truth.
- Pupils to discuss the difference between saying 'It is true that God exists' and 'It is true that the head teacher exists'. If there is a difference between the two, then can we use the same word 'true' for both?
- Pupils to look at the statements on the sheet and work out which statements are examples of which type of truth. Do any statements belong in more than one category?

  – Scientific: All mammals are warm-blooded. Water is made up of two parts hydrogen and one part oxygen. Water boils at 100 degrees Celcius. All teenagers are between 13 and 19.

  – Logic: All mammals are warm-blooded.

  – Moral: Murder is wrong. You should respect your parents.

  – Religious: Sikhs believe in one God. Murder is wrong. You should respect your parents.

  – Historical: The Battle of Hastings was in 1066. Jesus was a Jew.

  – Absolute: All the statements contained in moral and religious truths would be applicable here.

- Pupils to think about the difference between absolute and religious truths and provide examples of the overlaps.

- Pupils to think about which type of truth is nearest to our general understanding of the word truth. Which is furthest away? Why?
  Give opportunity for pupils to discuss whether they feel it is more appropriate to speak about 'truths' or 'truth claims'. This is of particular relevance to pupils who are postmodernists.

Learning objectives and outcomes

To consider what truth means.
To classify statements into different sorts of truths.

Synopsis

C1: A look at different meanings of the word truth.

Religious literacy: Words to be introduced – scientific truth, religious truth, historical truth, truths, absolute, logic, moral.

Prior learning: None necessary.

Links: History, science, maths, ethics, logic. See B12 *Is Hume correct?* in *Truth-Seekers: Thinking about God* for a more detailed look at the nature of scientific truths.

Pupils working at higher levels

- Pupils could write a fictional story (a couple of paragraphs long) that incorporates as many different uses of 'true' and 'truth' as possible. Pupils should focus on making a structured story – not simply writing random examples, such as the ones on the sheet.

- Pupils could grapple with the different types of 'truths' by taking one subject and making truth statements about the subject in as many different truth categories as possible. For instance, if the subject was Jesus pupils might assert that:

  – Historical truth: Jesus lived in the first century.

  – Absolute truth: Jesus is the Son of God (acccording to Christians).

  – Religious truth: 'I am the way, the truth, and the light' (John 3:19).

  – Moral truth: 'Love thy neighbour'.

  – Logical truth: Jesus Christ is Messiah (*Christos* in Ancient Greek means anointed one, and Messiah also means anointed one.)

  – Scientific truth: the Turin shroud is not from the time of Jesus.

- Pupils to analyse which types of truth are the hardest to find examples for, giving reasons why.

Pupils working at lower levels

- Pupils could monitor the discussion in their home for one or two days and write down examples of how their family/ teachers/friends use the word 'true'. This could be a homework task the week before starting the topic of truth.

- Pupils to take a newspaper page and highlight/extract as many different types of truth as possible. In groups of six, one student could be responsible for identifying each type of truth. (However, logical truths might be very difficult to find; teachers may want to find a suitable news page that includes some logical statements, or leave logic out.)

- Pupils working at lower levels could be given easier examples of truths to identify, such as historical truths.

Background: We commonly understand truth as being anything that accurately describes reality. However, our grasp on whether reality has been captured accurately can often be less than certain. In turn this will affect the word truth as used in different settings. Logical truths are true by definition – it cannot be false that all unmarried men are bachelors, because of the way we define the word bachelor. There is no possibility of error. Scientific truths can be tested by observation – it is a true fact that water boils at 100 degrees Celsius. However, with scientific truth, as truth is based on gathering sense data, there is always a possibility of error, however slim that might be. In the case of water boiling, that fact holds true in most cases. However, water boils at lower temperatures in places of high altitude. What we thought was a truth has been contradicted by finding an exception to the rule. There are many other examples of scientific truths that have been overturned due to new evidence, (for example, astronomy pre-Copernican revolution and the erroneous identification of phlogiston). See Background notes for moral (C2 **Absolutely true?**), religious (C7 **Can you belong to more than one religion?**, and 1 + 1 = 3 (C9 **How are religious truth claims different from other claims to truth?**) truths.

Teacher's notes: 1. What is truth?

Suggested teaching activities

C2 Absolutely true?

- For this activity, furniture should be moved so that there is a large space in the centre of the room for pupils to move around in freely. The following signs should be displayed around the room: 'Strongly disagree', 'Agree', 'Disagree', 'Not sure', 'Confused'.

Pupils should listen to various statements, such as the ones below, and then move to a particular spot, giving justify why they have moved to a particular spot, giving evidence wherever possible. Other pupils may change their minds as they hear the justifications for a position.

Guide pupils (who will want to discuss the issue) to discussing the broader picture of whether this is an example of an absolute truth, where people are wrong, or whether in a particular instance there is no truth.

  – It is true that abortion can never be justified.
  – It is true that we should honour our parents.
  – It is true that we should never steal.
  – It is true that we are all responsible for alleviating suffering.
  – It is true that we should never lie.

This should be followed up by a discussion about moral truth. Given the anticipated widespread difference in the class, are some people wrong and some right, or is there no such thing as moral truth? What reasons do pupils give for their answers?

- Teachers could use the activity sheet to provide thinking time prior to the above activity, or alternatively it could be used instead of the activity. Pupils should fill in the table on the page, which gives examples of nine actions. Pupils are to decide whether they think the action is always right or always wrong, or whether it depends on the situation. If they decide it depends, then pupils write down why. Similarly, they should be able to defend why they think it is always right or wrong if they believe that.

- Pupils could discuss whether the fact that moral codes are broadly similar across the world (and similar to most of the Ten Commandments) gives weight to the idea of a moral truth.

- Pupils to think about how a moral truth differs from a factual truth.

Learning objectives and outcomes

To give an informed personal response to whether there is such a thing as moral truth.

Synopsis

C2: Is there any such thing as moral truth?

Pupils discuss statements and how this impacts on their belief about truth.

Religious literacy: Words to be introduced – fact, evidence, moral, absolute, influence.

Prior learning: None necessary.

Links: The moral argument for the existence of God, ethics.

Background: Moral truths are claims that an action or intention is right or wrong. Specifically, moral realism states that these truths exist independently of our belief that the act or intention is right or wrong. Supporters of moral realism often refer to the fact that in broad terms ethical standards are similar across the world. Others rely on a moral lawgiver, usually God, to give grounding for moral creeds. Others disagree that morality is objective and static, and argue that morality is relative to culture, conditions and circumstances. Moral relativists would deny the existence of 'moral truths', although moral relativists are not a homogeneous group. An action is right for a utilitarian if it brings about the greatest happiness for the greatest number of people. Other moral relativists look to the consequences, rather than the intention of an action, to determine whether it is right or wrong. Something is right for supporters of situation ethics if it is the most loving thing to do in a given situation.

Where there is only one correct version of the truth, this is known as an absolute truth. Here it is believed that not only are truths independent of perception, but there is one correct version that exists to the exclusion of others. Religious truths often cross into this category ('No one gets to the Father, except through me' – John 14:6–9), as do some moral truths.

Pupils working at higher levels

- Pupils to define what 'moral truth' actually means, perhaps by using a community of enquiry approach (see p. 4).

- Pupils might like to consider and respond to this paradox: It is true that there is no such thing as 'true' in ethics.

- Pupils to analyse where their moral framework comes from. Pupils could make their own moral code, under the headings 'I would never do that!' and 'I strive to …'. Pupils should explain their influences for each of these.

- Give pupils a dilemma scenario such as ones found in *Sophie's Choice* (William Styron) or *The Cruel Sea* (Nicholas Monsarrat). How would they make their decision? Who/what would they want to consult before taking an action?

- Pupils to discuss: If there are no moral absolutes, then what are the consequences that arise from this for society and individuals?

- Pupils to research consequentialist theories of ethics. See http://plato.stanford.edu/entries/consequentialism

Pupils working at lower levels

- Pupils could do an exercise to acknowledge what influences their moral positions. They could look at a list similar to the following:

1 Stealing a pen from a friend.
2 Not returning a pen from a teacher.
3 Bullying a younger child.
4 Fighting a bully.
5 Gossiping about someone in your year.
6 Gossiping about a celebrity.
7 Not doing homework.
8 Staying out later than your curfew.
9 Not cleaning your room.
10 Staying up late, when your parents have told you to go to bed.

Depending on the aim of the activity, ability and age, pupils could do some of the following:

– Write down which ones they would do and would not do, giving reasons.
– Alongside reasons given above, pupils write down where they get their moral guidelines from: family/friends/society/religion /magazines/television, etc.
– Are any of their influences better than others? Why?

Teacher's notes: 1. What is truth?

Suggested teaching activities

C3 *Take the truth challenge*

- Pupils to read through the sections defining realism and postmodern perspectives on truth. Check understanding before pupils begin the questionnaire.
- Pupils complete the questionnaire and work out their score.
- Pupils to work in pairs, explaining to their partner the reasons they hold for being a realist or a postmodernist (either for individual aspects or overall).

Any one of the questions in this challenge can be used as a basis of an in-depth class discussion or debate.

C4 *What is truth like?*

- This sheet has various images that could represent different understandings of truth. Pupils could choose one picture (find/draw their own example that represents their understanding of truth), explaining why they chose that picture. Some pupils could build or elaborate on the image, e.g. the mirror could be broken if pupils wanted to show that reality is not reflected in the words we use to describe it.

The class/groups could make a poster to show the different understandings of truth. Pupils can label these appropriately. Examples could include:

- Elephant – We have access to partial truth (in reference to the poem about the six wise men of Hindustan, http://homepage.usask.ca/~wae123/misc/prose/hinustan.htm).
- Mirror – truth is reflected.
- Distorted mirror – truth is distorted by perception.
- Gold medal – one winner.
- Sunglasses – we see truth through different lenses.
- Picture – capturing reality accurately (or at an angle).
- Jigsaw – postmodernism.

Learning objectives and outcomes

To understand the difference between realist and postmodern perspectives on truth.

To give a personal response to questions of truth in ethics, aesthetics, religion and of the future.

To justify a personal perspective on truth.

Synopsis

C3: Are you a realist or a postmodernist about truth?

Take this questionnaire and see whether you have realist or postmodernist leanings.

C4: Pictures on truth.

Can pictures help us to access and develop understanding of the different interpretations of 'truth'?

Religious literacy: Words to be introduced – truth, postmodernism, realism, perspectives, constructed.

Prior learning: C2 Absolutely true?

Links: C10 In the eye of the beholder, C2 Absolutely true?

Pupils working at higher levels

C3 Take the truth challenge

- Pupils to debate: 'Without a realist perspective on ethics, anything goes'.
- Pupils to find contemporary quotes on truth and display them. These could be researched and taken from the world of media – music lyrics, interviews, films, etc. Pupils to match up the contemporary views with some of the views on the sheet (from people long gone).

C4 What is truth like?

- Pupils can research what different religions/religious leaders say about truth. Which religions have a similar outlook? Pupils could use sheet C4 and pick out pictures that represent that view of truth.

Pupils working at lower levels

C3 Take the truth challenge

- Some pupils will find concrete examples helpful when getting to grips with postmodernism. For example, the teacher could place an object, such as an exercise book, on a table and then make the claim 'The book is low down, in the left-hand side of the room.' Teachers should ask for four volunteers. One should crouch down on the ground near the book, two stand either side of the book, and one stands on a chair over the book. These pupils now answer the teachers' initial question. This could lead into a whole class discussion, or the questionnaire.

Background: It is hard to reach a definitive definition of postmodernism accepted by all. However, the relationship between postmodernism and truth is easier to pin down. Postmodernism affirms that there is no absolute truth. Instead truths are relative to the constructs of the framework that we operate in. We all operate within context-laden frameworks. Therefore, for postmodernists and other relativists, we are educated into believing truths, not discovering truths that are out there'. Anti-realism is a specific postmodernist theory of truth. It maintains that a statement is true, not because it corresponds with reality, but because it coheres with other beliefs within a form of life. Wittgenstein explained that language expressed a form of life; it is a human construct and as such does not attempt to mirror life. By contrast, realism maintains that a statement is true if it corresponds with the state of affairs it attempts to describe. Unlike anti-realism, truth does not depend on the society, the language or context. Instead, language tries to express reality, which lies beyond it, independent of observers and participants. Realism affirms bivalence. This principle states that every proposition must take one of two truth values – true or falsity, independent of any available evidence. Therefore, the statement 'There are green aliens on the planet Zig' is true now, if, and only if, there are green aliens on the planet Zig. Note that realists acknowledge that mistakes can occur. We may claim that it is not true that the planet Zig exists within our galaxy. We may back up this claim with evidence that there is not another planet in the galaxy that can maintain life. However, a realist will always be humble about the truth claims made – a mistake is always possible as it is impossible to know if all possible means of verification have been exhausted.

Note that it is possible to be a realist about some things and postmodernist about other things. For example, I might be a realist about ethics (e.g. the claim that 'murder is wrong' will either be true or false, independent of cultural beliefs) and take a postmodernist stance about other things, such as aesthetics.

Teacher's notes: 1. What is truth?

Suggested teaching activities

C5 Truth quotes

- Pupils to read through these quotes. These quotes can be used in different ways.
  - Pupils could explain what the quotes mean.
  - Split the quotes into those they agree with and those they disagree with.
  - Split them into realist and anti-realist understandings of truth.
  - Rank quotes in a diamond nine formation (with quotes at the top most reflecting what truth is like).
  - Find examples to back up each quote.
  - Find quotes that are compatible with a religious understanding of truth.
  - Split the quotes into paired opposites.
  - Match images from C4 **What is truth like?** to the quote sheet, C5.

Quotations can be differentiated to suit ability level. Those quotes in a box with a solid border are suitable for the majority of pupils to examine; those suitable for older or more able pupils have a dashed line border; those suitable for pupils at lower levels have a dotted border.

Learning objectives and outcomes

To reflect and give a personal response to the question: What is truth?

To choose/make symbols to represent different ways to understand truth.

Synopsis

C5: Quotes on truth. Can statements about truth enlighten us to the nature of truth?

Pupils working at higher levels

Quotations suitable for older or more able pupils can be recognised by a dashed line border.

Two longer quotations to discuss:

'A man may be a heretic in the truth; and if he believes things only because his pastor says so, or the assembly so determine, without knowing other reason, though his belief be true, yet the very truth he holds becomes his heresy' (John Milton).

'He who begins by loving Christianity better than Truth, will proceed by loving his own sect or Church better than Christianity, and end loving himself better than all' (Samuel Taylor Coleridge).

- Pupils to research the life of a person quoted to see if they lived by their understanding of truth. Teachers might want to limit this to particular individuals (such as religious leaders, philosophers, or scientists), or provide a limited number of quotes to choose from.

Pupils working at lower levels

C5 Truth quotes

- Teachers might like to cut the quotes up, giving one or two quotes to each pair to discuss. In their discussion, they should explain the quote and say if they agree or disagree, giving their reasons.

Quotations suitable for pupils working at lower levels can be distinguished by a dotted border. Teachers may have to explain who Plato was.

- Pupils could read the page and highlight any quotes they do not understand. These can then be shared and the meanings teased out by the class.

- Pupils to choose one quote on truth that best represents their understanding of truth and stick that into their book. They should explain why they chose the quote. The quote could be relevantly illustrated. The quote sheet could be sent around the class, with pupils signing their name next to the quote that best represents them. This could be displayed.

Teacher's notes: 2. Can conflicting truth claims all be true?

Suggested teaching activities

C6 Can everybody be right?

- Pupils could form a community of enquiry and share their personal opinions on a social, community, ethical or political topic. If interrupting is an issue, pupils might like to pass round an object, such as a Koosh ball, only speaking when they hold the object. They must take care to ensure they speak respectfully and every pupil must have an opportunity to share their views.

  When all the views have been shared, pupils should reflect on the discussion; in particular whether all opinions are true. Pupils should explain why or why not.

- Pupils to read the dialogue between Peter and George on the sheet and discuss the following:

  – Is George right when he says that they both can be right? If so, in what way are they both right?
  – How would you respond to George and Peter?

- Pupils to look at the three statements on the sheet. For each statement, they should tell a partner the opposite view, i.e. The earth is spherical. Astronauts have not landed on the moon. Adam was not the first human on earth.

  Pupils to consider whether they can hold both the statement and the opposing statement together as true.

- Pupils to discuss and respond to opposing and conflicting religious truth claims. Can religious claims that are in direct conflict with each other be correct? If not, then how do we work out which religious truth claims are correct?

Background: In a desire for tolerance, pupils often show reluctance to analyse beliefs critically, even when they are contradictory. Activity sheet C6 aims to raise questions about the nature of truth and whether all beliefs are valid. C6–C9 are concerned with truth explicitly, and tolerance implicitly. Good RE will represent each religion as faithfully and as accurately as possible, preserving the integrity of the religion. Inevitably, this will mean that pupils will need to grapple with the various truth claims made by each religion. While many religions share similarities of practice and intention, often truth claims in one religion will directly conflict with those in another. Pupils need to develop the skill of sensitively evaluating truth claims for themselves, while showing open-mindedness and tolerance. This will be very difficult for some pupils, but this essential skill can develop over time with practice. Often pupils will mistake evaluation for intolerance, and teachers may have to explicitly explain the difference.

The term 'religious pluralism' has been used with several different

Learning objectives and outcomes

To consider whether mutually conflicting claims can both be correct.

To give a personal response to the question of whether truth can be relative.

Synopsis

C6: Can all claims to truth by different religions be true?

George and Peter are in disagreement over the facts. They are both trustworthy. Can they both be right?

meanings. Pluralism is often used as a synonym for religious diversity. Sometimes pluralism can be used to denote that all religious truth claims are equally valid. However, this naive view of pluralism is not commonly accepted unqualified. A more sophisticated understanding of pluralism comes from theologian John Hick: 'In its broadest terms this is the belief that no one religion has a monopoly of the truth or of the life that leads to salvation' (http://johnhick.org.uk/article11.html). Hick maintains that there are no contradictions between truth claims as the truth claims are about different manifestations of God (or 'The Real'). These manifestations are to be understood in the context of the different cultures, languages and historical periods in which they arose. Revelation is therefore subject to interpretation and acknowledgement of the context. Of particular emphasis here is the ineffable nature of God (although Islam maintains that the Qu'ran was divinely revealed). For more information about pluralism see Hick, *An Interpretation of Religion.*

Pupils working at higher levels

- Pupils can research what a paradox is and some examples. Then pupils can invent their own paradoxes.

- Pupils to tease out the meaning and implications of respectful dialogue in the classroom. Does it leave room for disagreement?

- Pupils could write a 'Guide for Disagreement' for their class or a younger class.

- To what extent should we respect everybody's right to an opinion? (Does this include racist people, who seek to share religious or racist inflammatory comments?) Should we censure views that will be aired:

  – On TV?
  – Newspapers?
  – In school?
  – In Parliament?

Pupils working at lower levels

- Pupils could do an improvised role-play or write an imaginative piece about a place where no one ever disagreed with each other. Emphasis should be placed on showing the consequences of such a place.

  Pupils could choose one of the following open sentences:

  Alex: 'I think that we should take the one on the left.'
  Sam: 'I believe that the new school uniform should look like…'
  Kim: 'Yes, the situation is terrible. I think we should…'

- Pupils to think about when disagreement might be a healthy (or essential) thing. For instance, it might be helpful to disagree on people we find attractive! Pupils could explain why.

- Pupils to discuss the difference between disagreement and disrespect, using a Venn diagram. Pupils write words that are associated with disagreement on one side, and with disrespect on the other. They can use the overlapping section for any words that fit into both categories. Pupils to look over their completed Venn diagram and in pairs attempt to define the words 'disagreement' and 'disrespect'. During feedback, pupils should clarify the difference between the two words.

Teacher's notes: 2. Can conflicting truth claims all be true?

Suggested teaching activities

C7 Can you belong to more than one religion?

This activity is based on the book *The Life of Pi* (see Background). Although it would be profitable to read excerpts in class/homework, it is not necessary that teachers or pupils do so.

- Pupils to reflect and make a written response to whether they think they can belong to more than one religion, as part of a formative assessment.

- Pupils to discuss Pi's comment. Is religious belonging similar to nationality? Pupils could do a brainstorm of similarities and differences.

- Pupils write from the perspectives of Ravi, Pi, his parents and the religious leaders.

- Alternatively, pupils could role-play one/all of the following dialogues between:
  – Pi and Pi's mother.
  – Pi and either priest, pandit or imam (or all four if in a group).
  – Ravi and Pi.

The starting point for the role-plays is the text/speech on the page.

- In small groups, pupils could discuss whether it is possible to believe in more than one religion. *C8 Discussion grid* and guidelines for group discussion (A13) could be used to help pupils. See p. 19 for information on using the grid.

- Pupils to discuss who has missed the point, Pi, or the people he disagrees with. Pupils should explain their answers in full.

- Pupils could explore their understanding of religious truth claims through placing them on a Venn diagram. Pupils should then look at their diagram to see if there are any beliefs in one religion that are contradicted by a belief in another religion. If there are, then is it possible for more than one religion to be true?

- *The Life of Pi* is a good entry point for discussing what it means to belong to a religion.

Learning objectives and outcomes

To consider the case for religious pluralism.

Synopsis

C7: Considers whether religious pluralism is possible, and the difficulties of holding different sets of beliefs.

In *The Life of Pi*, by Yann Martel, Pi becomes a Hindu, Christian and Muslim at the same time.

Is this really possible?

How important are truth claims?

Religious literacy: Words to be introduced – tolerance, truth claims, inter-faith dialogue, disagreement.

Words that could be introduced at higher levels – integrity, pluralism.

Prior learning: None necessary, although familiarity with Venn diagrams is an advantage. It will also be advantageous for pupils to know some key beliefs for Christianity, Hinduism and Islam. This could be achieved as part of a research unit.

Links: Citizenship – belonging.

Pupils working at higher levels

- Pupils to produce a guide for interfaith dialogue for both faith and secular groups. This booklet should explain why interfaith dialogue is important, and how to sensibly discuss truth claims with people of other faiths.

- During the role-plays based on *The Life of Pi*, pupils should be encouraged to focus specifically on the religious beliefs of Christianity, Hinduism and Islam.

- Pupils to research what pluralism is, and which religions advocate pluralism. (This is difficult to generalise, as many believers will have their own opinions. However, some branches of Hinduism and Sikhism advocate pluralism. See Introduction to the unit, p. 54). Pupils can discuss the merits of pluralism and any drawbacks.

By reading more of the book, pupils could explore Pi's reasons for joining all three religions. They could write a report on whether Pi was fundamentally mistaken in his belief that he could join all three.

Pupils working at lower levels

- It will be helpful for some pupils to have phrases to use in discussions to show that they respectfully disagree with each other. They could make their own posters to place at eye level, or in the front cover of their book. Some phrases that pupils might want to include are:

  – I disagree because . . . .
  – Why do you think that?
  – I think something different. . .
  – What evidence have you?
  – I believe . . .
  – Some Muslims/Sikhs/Jews . . .
  – My reasons are . . .

Before pupils discuss truth claims, it will help if they have practice using these phrases on a topic less controversial! This might be an ethical or social issue, such as the ones in C2 **Absolutely true?**

- Pupils could do a quick warm-up activity in groups, finding as many ways to disagree with someone as politely as they can, without using the word disagree.

---

practises at the temple, church and mosque. This is met by an appalling display of religious intolerance between the three leaders, and cold disapproval. The section concludes with Pi continuing to practise all three religions, although he can no longer go to his parish church, he changes his prayer times in the temple and he cannot linger with his fellow Muslims after Friday prayers. Pi feels that the religious leaders have all missed the point. Although the pandit, priest and imam behave poorly in the book, it does raise the question of whether truth claims are essential to religion, and whether pluralism can work.

Background: Activity sheet **C7** is based on the book, *The Life of Pi*, by Yann Martel. This book is accessible for most pupils with a reading age of 13+. Between chapters 15 and 28, Pi (a 14- year-old boy living in Pondicherry, India) seeks God and finds him in Hinduism, Christianity and a year later in Islam. This section of the book deals with whether it is possible to belong to more than one religion. Pi, who just wants to 'love God', sees no problem in this, as each religion offers him a different access point to God. The pandit, priest and imam, however, disagree. In a chance meeting with Pi and his parents (p. 64), they discover that Pi

Teacher's notes: 2. Can conflicting truth claims all be true?

Suggested teaching activities

C9 How are religious truth claims different from other claims to truth?

- Pupils to read the first box on the sheet and discuss the difficulties of testing religious truth claims. Pupils might be given a range of truth claims as a stimulus, such as: Reincarnation; Jesus' resurrection; the existence of God; Allah created Adam from a clot of blood; the Trinity; Sikhs should engage in service to others; nirvana.

  Pupils could take one truth claim and decide whether it could be tested. If it could, then pupils to suggest what tests might be applicable. If the truth claim is not open to testing, pupils to explain why not.

  Pupils to discuss: If religious truth claims are not open to testing, then how do we know that they are real?

- In pairs, pupils to read the dialogue about the Trinity.

- Pupils to look at the symbolic explanations of the Trinity (a)–(f) and decide whether these are good explanations, giving reasons for their answers. Teachers to draw out in discussion to what extent our language, symbolic or literal, can successfully describe things of a religious nature.

- Pupils to discuss in what ways religious truth claims differ from other truth claims/scientific truth claims?

  Teachers could then introduce the concept of a 'leap of faith' as a characteristic of many religious beliefs (see Background).

- Pupils to read the story of Abraham in Genesis 22:1–18 (**C9 ext** on the CD-ROM). If this story is presented on an A4 sheet, pupils can annotate the margins of the sheet with questions relating to aspects they find interesting or puzzling, or questions they would want to ask Abraham or Isaac.

  Pupils to discuss:
  – Whether they could have had the same level of faith as Abraham, explaining why or why not.
  – Whether Abraham was right to maintain his faith and sacrifice Isaac to God. (Pupils may like to look at Genesis 17 first, where Abraham encounters God for the first time.)

- Would you be prepared to take a leap of faith for anything/anyone? Pupils to explain their reasons.

Learning objectives and outcomes

To understand that religious truths are different from other types of truths.

To understand that many religious truths are explained symbolically.

To recognise the limitations of symbols or comparisons in explaining religious truth claims.

Synopsis

C9: Explores the mystery of the Trinity.

The Trinity is One God with three persons. But what does this really mean?

Religious literacy: Words to be introduced – Trinity, substance, essence, leap of faith.

Prior learning: None necessary.

Links: B1 Knowing God in *Truth-Seekers: Thinking about God*; Unit A: The theory of knowledge in this book.

Pupils working at higher levels

- Pupils to look at the Ancient Greek words used to describe the Trinity: *prosopon* (face, mask) and *ousia* (substance, essence). Do these words help us to explain the Trinity?

- Pupils could work in pairs and challenge each other to describe impossible things, e.g. a square circle.

- Pupils to explain why our language strains when trying to describe some religious beliefs.

- Pupils to think of examples where symbols can be misinterpreted. Pupils could start with road signs, imagining a stranger unfamiliar with such signs coming across them for the first time. How might the signs be interpreted?

Pupils working at lower levels

- To explore the question at the bottom of the worksheet, pupils could draw a Venn diagram, with 'scientific truth' in one circle and 'religious truth' in the other circle. In pairs, pupils to brainstorm words associated with truth. They should then write these within the relevant circle; aspects where scientific and religious truth are the same can go in the overlapping segment. Pupils can then brainstorm religious and scientific truths separately, adding the words to the diagram.

- In comparing religious and scientific truth claims, teachers may like to provide pupils with specific examples of each to stimulate thinking e.g. 'Water boils at 100°C'; 'The Qur'an was revealed to Muhammad (pbuh) by the Angel Jibril.'

Background: The doctrine of the Trinity states that God is one being or substance (the ancient Greek term is *ousia*) who exists as three fully divine persons, Father, Son and Holy Spirit. These persons are identical and indivisible in essence, yet are distinct from each other. The doctrine also teaches that the second person of the Trinity, the Son, has a fully human nature and a fully divine nature (hypostatic union). The term 'person', when used of the Trinity, has a different meaning from our understanding of the word. The Greek word was *prosopon*. This can be translated as 'face' or 'mask', and relates better to the word 'persona' than the word person.

The doctrine of the Trinity, like many other religious creeds and doctrines, is mysterious. While we can accept that Christians believe that God is three in one, in reality it is impossible to grasp what it might mean for God to be three and one simultaneously. In this sense, many religious beliefs lie beyond rational discourse and so rely on faith. Reason can take us only so far. Søren Kierkegaard makes the point that we cannot bridge the gap between our finite, limited and mundane understanding and what is infinite and extra-mundane. Therefore, the only thing that can bridge the gap is a leap of faith. An essential element here is that the leap is uncertain – that is what characterises faith. Kierkegaard stated that religious truths are subjective. In this they are properly known only through the experience of living one's life, and the feelings we have about it.

Not all religious believers would agree with Kierkegaard. Many would argue that while they are prepared to take a leap of faith, the basis of their belief is not groundless, but based on knowledge gained from revelation and intuition.

Teacher's notes: 3. Is truth just a matter of perspective?

Suggested teaching activities

C10 In the eye of the beholder

- Pupils to read Merry's story and consider whether Merry was wrong in finding the dinosaur beautiful.

- Pupils to think about the meaning of the quote 'beauty is in the eye of the beholder'. Do pupils agree that beauty is subjective?

- Pupils could do the activity on the page that asks them to list, rank and compare beautiful things. Or they could do the physical version be ow.

- Pupils to do a concept line activity where they place themselves in a line according to whether they find something beautiful or not. One end should be labelled 'extremely beautiful' and the other end labelled 'extremely ugly'. Teachers can use objects, artwork, pieces of poetry, pictures of famous people, and tasting foods as stimuli. It is important that the results are followed up with questions, such as:

  What influences our perceptions of beauty? If we disagree, does that necessarily mean that there are multiple truths? Is there a truth tc be found when it comes to beauty?

  If pupils think that there is no truth to be found when it comes to beauty, then move on to discuss music or morality.

- For a homework task, pupils could write a short descriptive piece titled 'My room'. This should be from their point of view. They could tnen get someone else in their family to also write a short piece about the pupil's room. In class, pupils can discuss the differences between the two pieces. In what ways does this highlight the problems with reaching an understanding of truth?

- Pupils could discuss what 'inside' and 'outside' beauty are and whether one is 'more beautiful' than the other. Does this affect their understanding of the word beauty?

- Can photos capture the inner beauty of a thing? Teachers might like to hold an inner beauty photo challenge to find the inner beauty in unlikely places. Pupils could take photos in the school grounds or in a neighbouring area. To discuss: Can beauty be found in anything?

Learning objectives and outcomes

To reflect on whether beauty is subjective or objective.

Synopsis

C10: An introduction to relativism.

Merry, a toddler, was struck by the beauty of a dinosaur.

Pupils to look at whether we can say that it is true that some things are beautiful, or is beauty purely subjective?

Religious literacy: Words to be introduced – perspective, subjective, objective.

Words that could be introduced at higher levels – aesthetics, relativism, postmodernism.

Prior learning: None necessary.

Links: The moral argument, art, science, maths. *Truth-Seekers: Thinking about God:* **B8 Rose-coloured glasses, B14 Sounds convincing.** *Truth-Seekers: Thinking about God's Nature:* **B18 An anthropocentric world.**

Background: Postmodernism rejects truth as something real that can be discovered. Like other relativists, post modernists maintain that truth is relative to the perceiver. It is based on the notion that we cannot step outside from our standpoint to reach objectivity when making judgements. Some people are relativists about particular areas (such as beauty), while others are relativists about all things including knowledge. Realists (who affirm bivalence and believe that our language refers to a reality) reject the relativist claims, arguing that they must be an independent standpoint, even if we cannot always reach it, if all thought is not to be paralysed.

The saying 'beauty is in the eye of the beholder' is rephrased from Shakespeare, and found in Margaret Wolfe Hungerford's 1878 novel

Pupils working at higher levels

- Pupils could research psychological studies that suggest that physical beauty is not in the eye of the beholder. For instance, we do arguably find certain types of faces beautiful.

  Pupils might also like to research and then reflect upon how (and to what extent) Fibonacci's 'golden number' gives us insight into what beauty is (see Background).

- Pupils could bring in examples of natural/man-made beautiful things as stimulus for discussion.

- As an extension to considering the role of truth in beauty, pupils could look at art in a broader sense. Topics to examine could be:

  – Is beauty related to usefulness?

  – What is art?

  Pupils could look at a piece of modern art to see if they would (a) call it art; (b) call it beautiful; and whether there is a truth to be found regarding (a) or (b). In particular they might like to look at work by Tracey Emin (www.saatchi-gallery.co.uk/artists/tracey_emin. htm) or Rosalie Gascoigne (www. roslynoxley9.com.au/artists/15/ Rosalie_Gascoigne). Is the beauty in the art itself, the cleverness of the composition or intention, or the message that is communicated?

- Pupils could make their own modern art using found objects. For example, sculptures that express something (eternity, life, death, beauty, or perhaps truth itself).

Pupils working at lower levels

- Pupils to make a cartoon (role-play, storyboard or story) about seeing something through the eyes of a toddler and then through the eyes of an adult. (The story could be based in places such as a playground, kitchen, garden or supermarket.) On the basis of this, pupils to discuss whether this means that there is more than one 'truth'?

- Pupils could have a page of different images from the natural world as well as man-made objects. These could include the Eiffel Tower, scaffolding, a beautiful building such as a classical building or the Taj Mahal, a rose, a dandelion, a cactus, mountains, roads and snails.

  – Pupils could sort these into 'beautiful' and 'not beautiful' things. (Pupils to think about to what extent beauty is related to rare things.)

  – Pupils could discuss why the Eiffel Tower might be regarded as beautiful when it is basically scaffolding. If we put lights on other scaffolds would this make them beautiful? Pupils could compare a dandelion to a rose. Why is one regarded as a weed? Is one more valuable than the other?

Molly Bawn. Many people are relativist about aesthetics, although some people hold that there is an aesthetic truth to be discovered. Psychologists have done tests on people we find attractive, some concluding that the faces that we find more pleasing are symmetrical. Leonardo Fibonacci is famous for his sequence of numbers in which each number is the sum of the previous two. When each number is divided by that previous to it in the sequence, it gives a result of around 1.618, known as the golden ratio. This sequence occurs throughout nature (for example in the spiral pattern of a snail, the arrangements of seeds in a sunflower, the length of the foot in relation to distance to the knee and also the pelvis). The golden number has been used as the basis for many realist claims that there is an underlying truth in what we consider beautiful.

Teacher's notes: 4. Can we discover what is true?

Suggested teaching activities

C11 Digging deeper

- In this activity pupils are encouraged to ask questions. If we can critically examine what we are presented with, and we can clarify, justify, provide evidence for, confirm or reject what is being said, then we will be closer to reaching the truth.

- Pupils to read the sheet, which is a guide to asking basic questions. Pupils could be given a recent newspaper article with unanswered questions. Pupils to write down questions they would ask to get a fuller understanding/the truth.

Activities to help pupils deepen understanding through skills of observation

- Pupils to discuss/write what they noticed, last time they went down their street (or walk from the school gates to inside their classroom). Were they observant? Why or why not?

- Pupils to discuss their listening skills. Pupils to consider whether they ever 'switch off' while listening at school or home. What might the consequences of switching off be? How could we develop listening skills?

- Pupils to discuss what misunderstandings could occur between different religions if we do not listen carefully, be observant, or read with care? (Pupils could come up with their own examples.)

- Pupils to examine a picture and describe it in detail. Paintings by Bruegel the Elder are useful (religious and secular) as they are busy pictures with lots of details to find. Some of Bruegel's paintings can be found at www.nationalgallery.org.uk. One such picture attributed to Bruegel, 'Landscape with the Fall of Icarus', might be used effectively here. (www.mlahanas.de/Greeks/Mythology/Master3.html).
Pupils could study the picture, listing what they can see, and drawing conclusions about the meaning of the painting. Many pupils will fail to spot a pair of thrashing legs belonging to Icarus in the bottom right-hand corner, which gives context to the painting.

Pupils could formulate questions to help them discover what the painting is about, e.g. What is the shepherd doing? Whose legs are in the water? Why is no one helping/noticing the boy in the water? Pupils to predict/discuss possible answers.

- This exercise might also be done with a religious artefact. The artefact (which ideally will be unfamiliar to pupils) should be shown to the pupils, giving them all opportunities to observe carefully by looking (and touching if appropriate).

Pupils could then list everything they notice about the artefact before writing a list of questions about the artefact. Once questions have been written they can research and discuss the answers. This activity could scaffolded in a KWL chart. This is a three-columned chart with the headings Know, Want to know, Learned.

Learning objectives and outcomes

Use questions to search for meaning and truth. Critically examine texts.

Synopsis

C11: Uses questions to reach a deeper understanding.

Pupils use questions to look beneath the surface to see how we can get closer to the truth.

Pupils working at higher levels

- Philosophers have been accused of never getting to the bottom of an answer, but simply raising more questions than they started with. Assess the benefits and problems of using questioning as a tool to reach the truth.

- Pupils could discuss the A. N. Whitehead quote: *'Not ignorance, but ignorance of ignorance is the death of knowledge.'* How is this quote related to questioning and truth?

- Pupils could do some critical reasoning based around asking questions. They could take newspaper articles and highlight facts, opinions and reasoned judgements (see **A1 Fact, opinion, belief**).
After they have done this, they should generate questions in response to the opinions and reasoned judgements. They could research those answers and discuss to what extent it helped them grasp the truth of the situation.

- Pupils might discuss information about religions that they get in RE lessons/GCSE courses. Is this information similar to soundbites? Should there be less breadth and more depth? Does information gleaned in RE lessons ever distort the truth due to a shallow understanding? Can they find examples where a little bit of true information may lead to a lack of understanding and misinformation? What advice have pupils for exam boards?

Background: We are often fed compressed soundbites of news, as headlines, summaries, or updates. Some news programmes (such as CNN) run a ticker tape of news stories at the bottom of the screen which are compacted into a sentence or two. Can we say that these soundbites are giving us the truth? When information is trimmed and squeezed into such a small package, then does this necessarily lead to distortion of the truth? How much detail is necessary before we can say we have the truth? In education, there has always been tension between the breadth and the depth of coverage of a topic. In the late 1990s, the Singaporean government announced that the breadth of factual knowledge in the school curriculum would be cut by one-third to make way for more detailed understanding of the issues studied and the explicit teaching of thinking skills. Teaching pupils how to dig deeper is imperative if school leavers are to make sense of tomorrow's world. For more information on how questioning can be used effectively to gain deeper understanding, see Jamie McKenzie's website www.questioning.org.

Pupils working at lower levels

- Pupils can research an RE topic of their choice. For the planning stage, they could write down the name of the topic in the middle of an A3 piece of paper. Around this, they should write what they already know in a different colour. Around that they should write questions about what they want to discover (in another colour). Finally they should write questions coming off those questions, which highlight things they might have to take into consideration/methodology when looking at their first set of questions. When they have finished this they can begin their research.

They should make an ignorance log of all questions that come to mind when they are doing their research. They should formulate questions for any article or text they read to help them to critically assess it (see below).

- Pupils to go out onto the field/playground and find at least five things they have never noticed before. Pupils to share their findings.

- Pupils could make an observations log on a visit to a place of worship. They could write down all observations under different categories that the class construct together. In doing this, pupils should bear in mind the function and sanctity of the place of worship, as well as practical considerations.

Teacher's notes: 4. Can we discover what is true?

Suggested teaching activities

C12 Discovering truth

- Pupils to read the account of baptism. Accounts such as this one might be found in a standard textbook about Christianity. The account is factual and dry. Although there is nothing incorrect in the account, pupils should consider to what extent it tells us the whole truth about baptism. Pupils to log their questions.

- Pupils could answer the questions on the sheet. What questions would you want to ask to discover the truth? Why? Which people would you ask?

- The topic of discovering truth can be linked to questions about identity. Pupils could think about the truth about themselves and others in the class. On a blank page each pupil should draw an outline of themselves (not a stick person as pupils will need to write inside the outline). Pupils should then swap books with others in the class. Outside the outline of the person, pupils should write true and indisputable things about that person. When the pupils get their own books back, they could reflect in private writing or through discussion whether this has reached the 'truth' of who they really are. What has been left out? Why has it been left out? Pupils to work with a partner crafting some questions that when accurately answered could get closer to the truth about each other. Some pupils may wish to answer some of these questions as an extension.

- Pupils can examine pictures from a newspaper or a religious scene from a textbook. Why has the editor chosen this picture? What information does this picture communicate? What information/side of the issue has this picture left out? What picture scene would redress the balance?

- Pupils might discuss texting and the information they get sent via their mobile phone from outside agencies. Is the information ever misleading? Have they ever misunderstood a text, or has it ever misled them? What are the good points about texting and what are the bad points? What information is appropriate to text, and what is not? Why?

- Pupils can each be given an article without the headline, and try to sum it up in under eight words. Pupils to reflect on whether they think they have captured the truth. They should then tell their soundbite to a partner. Each partner could ask questions about the soundbite that would be necessary for them to understand the issue. What needs to be explained?

Learning objectives and outcomes

To understand that even true accounts can misrepresent the truth.

Synopsis

C12: Is basic (and partial) truth any better than no truth at all?

Even if we have true information, does it mean we have grasped 'the truth'?

Pupils working at higher levels

- Pupils to do a piece of writing about a topic that correctly informs on a superficial level, but does not get to the heart of the subject. Other pupils could then write some questions designed to dig deeper.

- Pupils to look at a few carefully chosen dictionary definitions and discuss how they do not 'capture' the truth about the subject. What would capture it?

- Pupils could study a historical event or religious story and then examine some paintings related to it. They could then discuss to what extent the artist has captured the event accurately. Pupils could discuss what has been left out, what angle the artist is taking and research why the artist has taken that angle. Many religious paintings related to Christianity can be found at www.nationalgallery.org.uk. Buddhist, Hindu and Jain paintings can be found at http://images.vam. ac.uk/indexplus/page/Home.html.

- Some pupils could create questions in order to discover the truth about who they are. To what extent do we know the truth about ourselves? Will we ever know ourselves properly?

- Pupils to look at the question: What is truth? This might be done as a community of enquiry, or as a discussion or an essay. Pupils might find it easier to start thinking about the topic by listing key words. Those experienced in questioning could begin by brainstorming questions that lead off this question. (For instance, is truth relative? How does perspective relate to truth?, etc.)

Pupils working at lower levels

- When questioning, weaker pupils might find it easier to start with the lower-order questions such as what, when and who, before progressing to how, which, would, why and should.

- Pupils to discuss which people they would ask to discover the truth about a particular belief. In the case of baptism, pupils might be given a list to choose from, e.g. imam, baptised teenager, a Maths teacher, an RE teacher, your parents, a Christian convert, a professor of theology, parents who are about to baptise their baby.

Pupils could pick out the top three people they would consider talking to, explaining their reasons.

Teacher's notes: 4. Can we discover what is true?

Suggested teaching activities

C13 What's at the heart?

This activity can be used with all religious and non-religious groups. It can also be easily adapted for use with religious and moral issues. The worksheet needs to be enlarged to A3 size, or preferably A2. If doing this activity as a whole class, rather than in groups, teachers may like to make their own version of the sheet to a suitable size.

- In groups of three or four, pupils brainstorm the beliefs, practices and objects related to one religion that they have studied. (The religion should be chosen by the teacher, and should be the same for the whole class.) The beliefs and practices should be summed up in one word, rather than in explanatory sentences (e.g. if the religion was Buddhism, pupils may have the terms mandala, meditation, teachings of Buddha, metta, among others). These should be written on small cards, or strips of paper. The emphasis here should be on the quantity of words produced. Each group should have about 30 words. Some teachers may like to share the words with the class, to ensure that each group has similar terms.

- Pupils then take turns within their group to place each card somewhere on the large sheet, according to the importance of the belief, practice or artefact. As they place the card they must justify where they are placing it, explaining their choice with a supporting reason. Pupils can decide not to place a card on the sheet, and instead move a card already on the sheet to a different place. Flexibility to debate the importance of an item, and move cards, is paramount here, so cards should be used rather than writing on the sheet.

Groups should write down their justifications for the cards they place at the heart of the religion.

When pupils have reached a consensus (or after a set amount of time), groups should pair up. Each paired group should swap places to analyse the other group's choices. After five minutes, each group to feed back to each other, highlighting inconsistencies or asking questions about choices. The other group gets a right of response.

Teachers should draw pupils' ideas together. The activity could be repeated for the whole class, or simply concentrate on what things lie at the heart of a religion (maximum of three things).

- For this activity to work, pupils need a good understanding of the topic/religion involved. It can be very fruitful for pupils to frequently evaluate their understanding in a chosen area – a belief system, or philosophical or ethical issue.

Pupils can reflect on their existing knowledge about a religious topic through the ranking exercise below. This will enable them to identify the next steps for developing knowledge.

The truth of the matter

- Pupils to draw a horizontal line. At one end of the line they write 'No understanding', and at the other end they write 'Complete understanding'. Between these pupils should write 'Shallow understanding', 'Reasonable understanding' and 'Deep understanding'. Pupils should brainstorm aspects of the topic or belief system first, then write these on the continuum at the appropriate place. Where they have evaluated their issue, belief or practice to lack deep understanding, pupils to write questions they need to answer to develop their understanding. Pupils can then research their questions.

Learning objectives and outcomes

To categorise beliefs and practices according to the importance accorded by the religion.

To identify what lies at the heart of a particular religion.

Synopsis

C13: Uses categorisation and ranking to help discover what is at the heart of a religion.

Pupils place beliefs and practices into four categories: Not important, has some importance, is very important, lies at the heart of the religion.

Religious literacy: Words to be introduced – compressed, distorted, expanded, soundbite, misinformation, mislead, accurate, assumption, clarity, precision, depth.

Prior learning: None necessary.

Links: A7 **How well do you know your stuff?**

Pupils working at higher levels

- Teachers choose a religion for the class to analyse.

In differentiated groups, pupils could be allotted specific categories for them to identify relevant key words. Pupils working at higher levels might be given categories that relate to more abstract beliefs, such as doctrine or dogma.

Teachers may wish pupils to work with or without textbooks, depending on ability, prior learning, and the context of this activity; whether it is to consolidate knowledge and understanding, or to develop knowledge and understanding.

- Pupils to discuss whether it is possible for us to gain complete understanding of something.

Pupils working at lower levels

- Teachers choose a religion for the class to analyse.

Teachers may like to provide appropriate textbooks for researching suitable words, rather than relying on prior learning.

In differentiated groups, pupils could be allotted specific categories for them to identify relevant key words. Pupils working at lower levels might be given categories with concrete facts to research, such as religious artefacts, festivals or places of pilgrimage.

Teacher's notes: 5. How important is truth?

Suggested teaching activities

C14 The last days of Socrates

- Pupils to read the sheet. This gives a brief overview of the charges brought against Socrates. For more detail see Background. Questions that could be discussed:
  - Were the charges brought against Socrates fair?
  - Was Socrates right or wrong to expose the lack of knowledge of prominent people?
  - To what extent is conscience a good guide in decision-making?
  - Why might Athenians have thought that Socrates, in asking the young to think for themselves and not blindly accept the ideas of their parents, was corrupting them?
  - Do you think that Socrates corrupted the young?
  - Why do you think that Socrates did not put on an elaborate defence? Should Socrates have put on a better defence?
  - Why do you think that Socrates did not suggest exile? Was he sensible in his suggestions for punishment? What would you have done in the same situation?
  - What would the consequences have been if Socrates had escaped to another land or was exiled?
  - Why do you think more people voted for him to be put to death than initially found him guilty?
- Pupils to read the extract from *Crito* on the sheet. Pupils to think or write about:
  - What arguments might Crito have for asking Socrates to escape?
  - What arguments might Socrates have for accepting his punishment?
- Pupils to prepare and act out a role-play based on this conversation and what they think is said next.
- Pupils to discuss whether they have more sympathy with Crito or with Socrates. What would they have done in the same situation?
- Pupils can look at the modern case of Sandra Loranger who was imprisoned in California in 1989 for feeding homeless people. Pupils can consider what the phrase 'living in the truth' means, and how important that is. Was Lcranger right to disobey the law? Pupils might speculate as to what Socrates would have done in the same situation.

Learning objectives and outcomes

To consider how important truth is, and to what extent you would defend the truth.

Synopsis

C14: Is the truth worth dying for?

Pupils look at (Socrates' friend) Crito's attempt to persuade Socrates to escape from prison and thus save his life.

Why did Socrates ignore him, and was he sensible to do so?

Religious literacy: Words to be introduced – truth, martyr, sacrifice, corruption, hypocrite.

Prior learning: None is necessary, although it would be helpful to have discussed truth with pupils.

Links: Citizenship – *Crito* raises the question of the rights of an individual and the extent of the individual's duty to obey the law.

Background: Plato discusses the last days of Socrates in *Crito*, *Phaedo* and *The Apology*. *The Apology* covers Socrates' trial; *Crito* deals with Socrates' refusal to escape from prison and thus save his life; *Phaedo* discusses the nature of the afterlife. A compilation of the Four Dialogues can be found in Plato, *The Trial and Death of Socrates: Four Dialogues*. The painting is by Jacques-Louis David ('The Death of Socrates'), 1787, Metropolitan Museum of Art, New York.
Sandra Loranger was imprisoned in California in July 1989 for 45 days for feeding the homeless. Loranger was given a choice of probation (where she was not allowed to feed the homeless) or imprisonment. She 'chose' imprisonment, saying, 'If feeding people is a crime, then I am beyond rehabilitation.'

Pupils working at higher levels

- Pupils could research modern or ancient martyrs who died as a consequence of defending or exposing the truth. Was their sacrifice worth it?
- Pupils to discuss how far they would go to defend the truth. Pupils could think about scenarios where the truth is challenged. (For instance, a child is wrongly accused of a misdemeanour and will get a larger punishment if they continue to protest their innocence.) Pupils to think up at least five different scenarios, in groups, and to feed back or lead a discussion on how they would react.
- Pupils to think about why truth is worth pursuing.
- Pupils to think about what truths they would want to defend and why.
- Pupils to discuss the following quote from Aristotle: 'I love Plato dearly, but truth dearer still.' (Plato was Aristotle's teacher.) What did Aristotle mean? Why might he have said this?
- Pupils could discuss the purpose of education. In particular, to what extent should we teach pupils to develop independent thought? (Some cultures would not see this as an aim of education.)
- Pupils could look at the arguments that Socrates makes in *Crito* against escaping the death penalty imposed on him by the law.
- Pupils with a reading and comprehension age of 15+ might like to read sections of *Crito*, *Phaedo* or *The Apology*. These are all accessible works of Plato.

Pupils working at lower levels

- Pupils could write creatively about a world where nobody told the truth about anything. Pupils should focus on the consequences of a world where the truth was unimportant.

  This creative piece could be in the form of a story, poem, rap or play. Pupils might like to act out their stories.

  This could be followed up with a discussion of why truth is important.

Teacher's notes: 5. How important is truth?

Suggested teaching activities

C15 Truth and reconciliation

- Pupils to read the sheet. Some pupils may not be aware what apartheid is, or the impact it had in South Africa and the world. Teachers may like to provide supplementary information.

Pupils could answer the questions on the sheet. Some pupils may need some structure for questions 3 and 4. In turn, pupils could brainstorm 'truth' and 'justice'. In their spider diagram, pupils should focus on why each value is essential. Alternatively, half the class could brainstorm 'truth' and the other half brainstorm 'justice'. A whole class feedback could precede pupils answering question 3.

- Pupils could hold a values auction to see which is the most prized value. Pupils to have a budget and to select and bid for particular values.

Pupils should pick their top five values, explaining why they would want to bid for these. Pupils should then work out a budget. What values would they like to own? How many will they try to bid for? What is the top price they are prepared to pay for one value? Then the bidding can commence with the teacher as auctioneer.

When everything has been sold, pupils can reflect on what they have ended up with. Did they make wise choices? Explain why or why not.

Extension

- Pupils should split into two groups. Both groups are to imagine that they are on the advisory board to Nelson Mandela, as he took up office as president. One group should prepare a case to show how justice is paramount in building a united South Africa. The other group should prepare a case to show how truth is the most essential in building a united South Africa.

These cases should be presented to the president. Each case should focus on consequences of not adopting truth or justice as a primary aim. Pupils could look to see examples in other parts of the world/history where truth or justice were regarded as essential.

Learning objectives and outcomes

To evaluate whether truth is more important than other values (such as justice).

Synopsis

C15: Is truth more important than anything else?

Post-apartheid, the Truth and Reconciliation Commission was set up to assign blame to individuals over apartheid atrocities. In return for a full confession, individuals were given partial impunity.

Religious literacy: Words to be introduced – truth, reconciliation, value, justice, apartheid.

Prior learning: None necessary.

Links: History, politics, ethics, values.

Pupils working at higher levels

C16 A deeper look at truth

This is a set of three extension tasks for pupils on issues surrounding truth, designed to be used separately.

Whose truth? Asks pupils to consider ways of discovering truth.

How do we know we have the truth? Covers issues of humility and the truth. It focuses on events in the life of Galileo. Pupils can discover more information about Galileo at *The Galileo Project* (http://galileo. rice.edu).

How important is the truth? Covers issues of integrity and the truth.

- Pupils can watch a clip from *The Matrix* where Neo and Morpheus meet. Morpheus offers Neo two pills: the red pill will give Neo the truth about the Matrix (and remove him from it). This course of action is risky and will undermine everything Neo thinks he knows. The blue pill by contrast offers him his old life, and certainty. Teachers should stop the clip after Morpheus says 'Remember, all I am offering is the truth. Nothing more.'

Pupils to discuss whether Neo should take the blue pill or the red pill. Is ignorance bliss? Would they take the blue or red pill, and why?

There are several essays on philosophy and *The Matrix* at http://whatisthematrix. warnerbros.com/rl_cmp/new_ phil_fr_intro.html.

Pupils working at lower levels

- Some pupils will benefit from a word bank to help them think through possible answers. Below are some relevant words and phrases that can be used for questions 1 and 2.

1 Prison, capital punishment, corporal punishment, apology, community service, pay, justice, suffer.

2 Right, wrong, misled, mistaken, good intentions, should, should not, considered all possibilities, take into account.

Background: The Truth and Reconciliation Commission was set up after apartheid ended. First, it was part of a compromise, which led to the end of apartheid. However, it was also felt that the commission was the best way forward for the country. Contrary to what many black leaders were expecting, it was felt that justice would not aid the healing of the nation. If the crimes committed under the name of apartheid were not acknowledged, and those who committed the crimes not identified, then the cycle of hurt, violence and retribution would continue. Truth was regarded as the key to progress, not justice. Getting officials to confess to their crimes was deemed a very difficult task, yet it was an essential one. However, if people were not afraid of imprisonment, then they would be more likely to come forward and accept responsibility for their crimes. Those who confessed in full and could show that their crime was politically motivated were granted partial (and in some cases full) impunity. This would help all South Africans to move on, as the perpetrators would take responsibility for their actions.

A simple report on the Truth and Reconciliation Commission in South Africa, with links to more detailed reports, can be found at http://news.bbc.co.uk/1/hi/world/africa/142369.stm. Other Truth and Reconciliation Commissions have been set up in other countries where there has been conflict. See the following links for more information: http://trcsierraleone.org/drwebsite/publish/intro.shtml (Sierra Leone); https://www.trcofliberia.org (Liberia); http://www.info.gov. za/otherdocs/2003/trc (South Africa); http://news.bbc.co.uk/1/hi/ special_report/1998/10/98/truth_and_reconciliation/203134.stm (Report on South Africa).

Teacher's notes: 5. How important is truth?

Suggested teaching activities

C17 And if it's true?

The activity sheet asks pupils to imagine that a belief that is important to them is proven. Pupils then predict the consequences of this new proof. The scenario is set with a newspaper article which breaks the news. Pupils to read through this passage. In order to answer the questions below, pupils need to follow the four steps at the bottom of the page.

Pupils could study the John Betjeman poem 'Christmas' from the sixth stanza onwards. This poem contrasts the rituals and frivolity of Christmas time with the Christian message, indicating that if this incarnation is true, then nothing compares to it, hinting at the impact of truth claims and the real demands of faith.

- With a teacher, pupils could discuss the extent to which our beliefs make an impact on our lives. Should all our beliefs affect the way we live our lives?

- Pupils could study the sixth and seventh stanzas from the John Betjeman poem 'Christmas' ('And is it true?' http://blue.carisenda.com/archives/cat_john_betjeman.html) Pupils could respond to Betjeman's question 'And is it true?' by reflecting on their own beliefs. What impact have their own beliefs (religious, non-religious, other life stance, ethical) had on the way they live their life? If they knew that their beliefs were true, would they change the way they live their life now?

  - Pupils to think about or write down their most important beliefs and brainstorm how they would change their lives if they knew the belief were true. To ensure that they properly engage, pupils should be encouraged to write down beliefs that are responses to ultimate questions, e.g. Is there a God? What happens to us when we die?

  - Pupils to consider whether other people's lives would change too.

- Pupils to research a person who has put faith into action. Suitable individuals might include: Mahatma Gandhi, Malcolm X, Martin Luther King, Oscar Romero, Ken Saro-Wiwa, Peter Singer. Pupils to explain how they put their faith into action.
  www.remembersarowiwa.com
  www.princeton.edu/~psinger
  www.cmgww.com/historic/malcolm/about/achievements.htm

- Pupils to consider ways in which they can get involved practically in putting their beliefs into action through active Citizenship.
  See www.globalgateway.org/Default.aspx?page=3109 for ideas.

C18 Summary

The two boxes offer summary notes. The first is an A5-size summary of Truth, Realism and Post-modernism that may be helpful revision for some pupils. It can be copied and stuck in an exercise book. There is also a list of key words for the unit. The list is not comprehensive and pupils can add to it.

Learning objectives and outcomes

To consider the relationship between belief and action.

Synopsis

C17: To what extent do beliefs change the way we live our lives? Should we do more to put our beliefs into action?

The belief pupils hold most dear to them has been factually proven. How does this change their lives?

Religious literacy: Words to be introduced – activist, civil disobedience, apathy.

Prior learning: None necessary.

Links: Active citizenship.

Pupils working at higher levels

- Pupils to reflect on the beliefs that are important to them. Do they already put their beliefs into action? If not, why not?
- Pupils could discuss some of the following and give a written response:
  - We are hypocrites about most of our beliefs.
  - Faith and action is such a powerful combination that it is inevitable that there will sometimes be bad outcomes.
  - Does faith justify any action? Discuss.
  - Can you truly believe in something and not yet change your actions in any way?

Pupils working at lower levels

- Pupils to write down/think about three important, personal beliefs. How do they show that they care about these beliefs?

Background: It is one thing to debate philosophically what it means for something to be true, and quite another to live by a truth claim or devote one's life to finding the truth. Yet many people swear by the truth, continue to fight for the truth, and are prepared to die for the truth. However, this is by no means universal. In an age where apathy is rife, it is all too easy to believe in something without the belief impinging on our lives. Pupils might be guided to research those individuals (both secular and theist) who have put beliefs into action.

C1 Is there more than one type of truth?

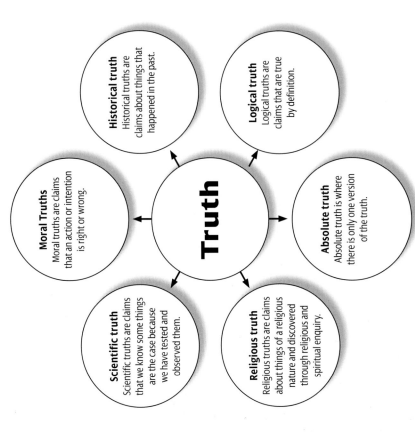

Truth

Scientific truth
Scientific truths are claims that we know some things are the case because we have tested and observed them.

Moral Truths
Moral truths are claims that an action or intention is right or wrong.

Historical truth
Historical truths are claims about things that happened in the past.

Religious truth
Religious truths are claims about things of a religious nature and discovered through religious and spiritual enquiry.

Logical truth
Logical truths are claims that are true by definition.

Absolute truth
Absolute truth is where there is only one version of the truth.

- Look at the statements below. Work out which statements are examples of which type of truth. Do any statements belong in more than one category?

1 All mammals are warm-blooded
2 Murder is wrong.
3 The Battle of Hastings was in 1066.
4 Sikhs believe in one God.
5 You should respect your parents.
6 Jesus was a Jew.
7 Water boils at 100 degrees Celcius.
8 All teenagers are between 13 and 19.
9 Water is made up of two parts hydrogen and one part oxygen.

C2 Absolutely true?

Is it true that moral actions, such as killing someone, are always right or always wrong? Someone who believes this is called an absolutist. Look at each of the actions below. If you think that it is true to say that the action is always right then tick the 'Always right' box. If you think that it is true to say that the action is always wrong, then tick the 'Always wrong' box. If you think that our judgement of the action depends on the particular situation, then explain your reason in the 'It depends' box.

Action	Always right	Always wrong	It depends on the situation
Disobeying your parents			
Always helping your little sister			
Breaking a school rule			
Defending your family or your friends			
Breaking a law			
Fighting			
Being honest			
Cheating			
Killing a person			
Stealing			

- Count up how many 'always right' and 'always wrong' answers you have. Count up how many 'it depends' answers you have. Are you an absolutist about moral truth?
- Is there any such thing as a 'moral truth'?
- How are 'moral truths' different from 'scientific truths'?

People use the term 'moral truth' to explain that some things are always right and some things are always wrong.

C3 Take the truth challenge

> Realists believe that when we say something is true, we are trying to express a true situation, independent of us, our society and language. Our belief corresponds with what is 'out there'.
>
> For some religious realists, beliefs reflect an absolute and complete truth.
>
> However, many realists about religion accept that our knowledge of the truth is partial. While our language tries to express our beliefs accurately, sometimes we have to use analogies and metaphors to do so.

> Postmodernists believe that there is no single truth. Instead, truth is constructed. Whether something is true will depend on the viewpoint from which it is being seen. Truth is relative to a culture, or language.

Approaches to truth... Are you a REALIST or a POSTMODERNIST?

• Are you a realist or a postmodernist? It is time to find out. Answer the multiple choice questions as honestly as you can. Ring the answer that is closest to what you believe.

Question 1 Your friends are having a disagreement. Aparna says that the Harry Potter books are the best ever. Ravi disagrees. What do you think?
(a) Aparna must be either right or wrong in her view about Harry Potter books.
(b) That there is no such thing as 'the best book'. It is all a matter of opinion.

Question 2 You watch Muslims file out from a mosque at the end of a service. They all believe in God, even though they cannot see God. What do you think?
(a) God is real for the Muslim community, it does not matter if in the end there is no God.
(b) It is either true or false that God exists. The answer is out there!

Question 3 You are heading off to the Glastonbury festival. Your dad doesn't understand why you like 'that music'. He says, "This is beyond doubt dreadful music.' Do you think that:
(a) There is no such thing as good music. It is just a matter of taste.
(b) Everybody's taste is different but really bad or really good music can be identified as bad. There are certain identifiable characteristics that make music bad or good.

Question 4 At the funfair you go to a fortune teller. She tells you that you will have 11 children by the time you are 38. What do you believe about fortune telling?
(a) It is true or false NOW that you will have 11 children by the time you are 38.
(b) It makes no sense to talk of how many children you will have by age 38 as it makes no sense to talk about things that have not happened yet.

C3 continues

C3 Take the truth challenge (continued)

Question 5 You are looking through a magazine and see a picture of someone you fancy. They were voted number 2 in a 'most beautiful person' poll last week. What do you believe about truth and beauty?
(a) Beauty is in the eye of the beholder. There is no such thing as universal beauty.
(b) It is true to say that some people are beautiful. There are certain characteristics that are universally regarded as 'beautiful'.

Question 6 You are studying ethics in RE. You learn that one reason that some people are vegetarian is because they believe animals have rights. You later take part in a heated argument about whether war can ever be justified. What do you believe about ethics and morality?
(a) Whether something is morally good or bad depends on the situation and the circumstance. Some moral codes are true for some people but wrong for others.
(b) There are certain moral codes that are true for all humans. We might not know what the truth is always, but there is an answer to whether something is morally good or bad.

Question 7 You are looking at world religions in RE. You read that Islam claims to have the truth. You also read that Christianity claims to have the truth. You read about Hinduism and Sikhism who claim that they partially know the truth. What do you believe?
(a) There is a truth to be found. All claims that religions make are true or false, even if we are not certain which ones are true at the moment.
(b) Each religion is true in all their beliefs. It does not matter that one religion's truth claims might contradict with that of another religion. As long as our beliefs about God fit in with other beliefs within the religion, it does not matter whether the belief exists in reality.

Now it is time to add up your answers! Look below and add up your realist and postmodernist answers.

1 (a) You are a realist about literature.
  (b) You are a postmodernist about literature.
2 (a) You are a postmodernist about God.
  (b) You are a realist about God.
3 (a) You are a postmodernist about music.
  (b) You are a realist about music.
4 (a) You are a realist about the future.
  (b) You are a postmodernist about the future.
5 (a) You are a postmodernist about beauty.
  (b) You are a realist about beauty.
6 (a) You are a postmodernist about ethics.
  (b) You are a realist about ethics.
7 (a) You are a realist about religious truth claims.
  (b) You are a postmodernist about truth claims.

• Can you explain to a partner why you are a realist or a postmodernist about particular truth claims?
• How might our beliefs about truth affect our beliefs about religions?

6 or 7 postmodernist points

You show the beliefs of a committed postmodernist. You tend to believe that beauty is in the eye of the beholder, and that we make our own truths (such as stealing is wrong). When we say something is true, we are saying that something is true in a particular context.

6 or 7 realist points

Ah. You are a clear realist about most matters. You tend to think that there is an answer for everything out there, even if we have not discovered it yet. You are unlike your postmodernist friends who believe that we make our own truths. . .

3–5 realist or postmodernist points

You are a realist about some truth claims and a postmodernist about others. For instance, you may believe that it is either true or false that there is life on Mars now, or that there are other planets. However, you may not believe that there is a truth to be known about the future (as it hasn't happened yet). You are likely to think that God either does or does not exist, but you are probably less clear as to whether it is true that your favourite band produces the best music in the world.

Truth-Seekers: **Thinking about Truth**

C5 Truth quotes

Read these quotes about truth.

- Choose two quotes and explain what they mean.
- Can you find examples that will explain these quotes?
- Which quotes do you agree with? Why?
- Are there any quotes that you strongly disagree with? Why?
- Can you split these quotes about truth into two or three different categories?

> The truth is always a compound of two half-truths, and you never reach it, because there is always something more to say.
>
> Tom Stoppard (b. 1937)

> Plato is dear to me, but truth is dearer still.
>
> Aristotle (c.384–c.322)

> A lie told often enough becomes the truth.
>
> Lenin (1870–1924)

> My great religion is a belief in the blood, the flesh, as being wiser than the intellect. We can go wrong in our minds. But what our blood feels and believes and says, is always true. The intellect is only a bit and a bridle.
>
> D. H. Lawrence (1885–1930)

> We also know how cruel the truth often is, and we wonder whether delusion is not more consoling.
>
> Henri Poincaré (1854–1912)

> The way I see it, it doesn't matter what you believe just so long as you're sincere.
>
> Charles M. Schultz (1922–2000) Creator of the cartoon 'Peanuts'

> All truths are easy to understand once they are discovered; the point is to discover them.
>
> Kahlil Gibran (1883–1931)

> Why, then, 'tis none to you; for there is nothing either good or bad, but thinking makes it so: to me it is a prison.
>
> William Shakespeare (*Hamlet*)/(1564–1616)

> The search for truth implies a duty. One must not conceal any part of what one has recognised to be true.
>
> Albert Einstein (1879–1955)

> And you will know the truth, and the truth will make you free.
>
> John 8:32

> I believe in everything – a little bit.
>
> Marilyn Monroe (1926–1962)

> Chase after truth like hell and you'll free yourself, even though you never touch its coat-tails.
>
> Clarence Darrow (1857–1938)

> Every man has a right to utter what he thinks truth, and every other man has a right to knock him down for it. Martyrdom is the test.
>
> Samuel Johnson (1709–84)

> Say not, 'I have found the truth,' but rather, 'I have found a truth.'
>
> Galileo Galilei (1564–1642)

Truth-Seekers: **Thinking about Truth**

C4 What is truth like?

- Look at the pictures.
  Which picture or pictures do you think represents truth the best?

Give your reasons why.

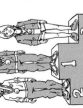
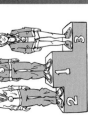
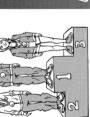
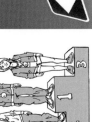

C6   Can everybody be right?

I respect George's opinions. We must both be right.

Peter never lies, and I never am wrong. Can it be true that it is *both* day and night?

Hello George, it is unusual to see you out in the daytime.

The daytime? Peter, don't you know that it is night-time at the moment!

- Look at the statements below. For each statement, give the opposite view.

The earth is flat.
Astronauts have landed on the moon.
Adam was the first human on earth.

Some people will disagree with the statements above, while others will agree. However, does this mean that both sets of people are right in their views?

- Can the statements above, and their opposite views, BOTH be true? Explain your answer.

We believe there is one God – Allah, and that prophet Muhammad (pbuh) is His messenger. We believe that Jesus was an earlier prophet. We call him Isa. We do not believe in the Trinity, although we believe that the holy spirit supported Isa (pbuh). We do not believe that Isa died on the cross.

I believe in Jesus Christ, the only Son of God. Jesus is part of the Trinity. This means that he is also part of God. The Trinity is three Gods in one – God the Father, God the Son and God the Holy Spirit.

I believe in G-d. I believe that no one is equal to G-d and no one can be part of G-d. I believe that Jesus was a Jewish teacher. I believe that he had and still has many followers, but I do not believe that he was G-d's son.

Can all claims to truth by different religions be true?
What happens when the claims conflict with each other?

C7   Can you belong to more than one religion?

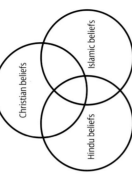

In *The Life of Pi* by Yann Martel, Pi decides to become a Christian, a Hindu and a Muslim, all at the same time.

The priest, pandit and imam disapprove, his brother Ravi mocks him, and his parents ask him to choose one religion out of the three.

'I don't see why I can't be all three. Mamaji has two passports. He's Indian and French. Why can't I be a Hindu, a Christian and a Muslim?'

Pi, speaking to his mother (p. 73)

'So, Swami Jesus, will you go to hajj this year? ... At the rate you're going, if you go to temple on Thursday, mosque on Friday, synagogue on Saturday and church on Sunday, you only need to convert to three more religions to be on holiday for the rest of your life.'

Ravi, speaking to Pi (p. 70)

- In groups, brainstorm Christian, Hindu and Muslim beliefs.

What beliefs do Muslims, Hindus and Christians share?

Christian beliefs

Islamic beliefs

Hindu beliefs

This is a Venn diagram. When completed it will show similarities and differences between Christian, Muslim and Hindu beliefs.

- Draw the Venn diagram on a large piece of paper.

- Fill in the centre of the Venn diagram with beliefs that Hindus, Christians and Muslims share.

- Fill in the sections between each pair of religions to show which beliefs they share with each other, but not the other religion.

- Finally, fill in the outer sections with beliefs that only that religion holds.

Look at your Venn diagram. Are there any beliefs in one religion that are contradicted by a belief in another religion?

- Do you think that it is possible to believe in more than one religion?

C9 How are religious truth claims different from other claims to truth?

If we want to test a scientific truth claim such as 'water boils at 100 degrees Celsius', it is clear what we have to do. We can conduct a fair test that shows the temperature that water boils at. However, if we make a religious truth claim such as 'God exists', then is it possible to conduct the same process of testing?

- What are the difficulties of testing religious truth claims?

Even if we cannot prove religious truth claims empirically, this does not necessarily mean that they are not true. (It may or may not be true that there is life in a different solar system. The reality is independent of the situation of whether we can test this to be the case.) One Christian truth claim that we cannot verify is the existence of the Trinity.

Christians believe that there is only one God, but God is made up of three persons. This is known as **the TRINITY**. Christians believe the Trinity is made up of the Father, the Son and the Holy Spirit. They each exist as distinct persons but are made up of the same substance.

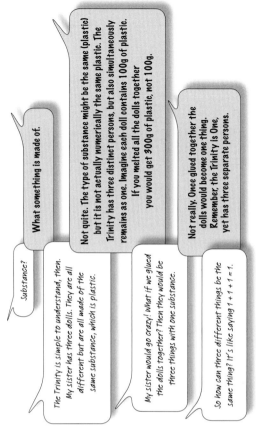

1+1+1 = 1?

Substance?

What something is made of.

The Trinity is simple to understand, then. My sister has three dolls. They are all different but are all made of the same substance, which is plastic.

Not quite. The type of substance might be the same (plastic) but it is not actually numerically the same plastic. The Trinity has three distinct persons, but also simultaneously remains as one. Imagine each doll contains 100g of plastic. If you melted all the dolls together you would get 300g of plastic, not 100g.

My sister would go crazy! What if we glued the dolls together? Then they would be three things with one substance.

Not really. Once glued together the dolls would become one thing. Remember, the Trinity is One, yet has three separate persons.

So how can three different things be the same thing? It's like saying 1 + 1 + 1 = 1.

Christians admit that it is hard to understand. Many Christians refer to the Trinity as a mystery, and often try to explain it through symbols or comparisons.

- Are these good explanations of the TRINITY?
  - (a) Like my cousins Bob, Job and Rob? They are identical triplets.
  - (b) A triangle – each angle represents one person in the Trinity.
  - (c)
  - (d)
  - (e)
  - (f)

- In what ways are religious truth claims, such as belief in the Trinity, different from other truth claims?

C8 Discussion grid
Can more than one religion be true?

Use this grid to help your group to discuss effectively. Follow the questions. Tick a box when a person from your group has spoken. Starred questions should be answered by each person in your group.

Initials of group members (one set of initials per column)						
*What do you initially think about this issue?						
*Why do you think this?						
In what ways are religions different from each other?						
Think of some examples from different religions to back up your points.						
Summarise the points made so far by the group.						
(Now everyone needs to write the summarised points in their books.)						
In what ways are religions similar to each other in their practices and beliefs?						
Do you agree that all religions are fundamentally the same?						
Can all religions lead to God?						
Summarise the points made so far by the group.						
(Everyone needs to write these points in their books.)						
*Is it possible to have many paths to one God?						
*Can more than one religion be true? Come to a group consensus.						
Write down your final answer and explain why you have agreed this as a group. What arguments did your group reject and why did they reject them?						

Truth-Seekers: **Thinking about Truth**

C11 Digging deeper

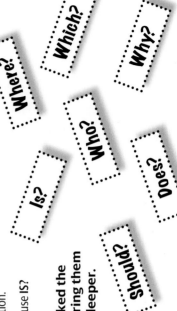

Sometimes it is hard to reach the truth. The truth can be covered up, or glossed over, or difficult to find, or even forgotten about. When we hear about issues, we might hear it through layers of opinion. When we are looking at a difficult or controversial issue, we need to be able to dig deeper in order to gain a proper understanding.

Before we can dig deeper, it helps if we know where to look. One way that might point us in the right direction is to ask some questions.

- If you need more information then you might ask a **WHAT?** question.

- If you want to know the place or the time, ask a **WHEN?** question.

- If you want to know the situation or location, you can ask a **WHERE?** question.

- If you are offered alternatives and need to make a choice, then it can help to ask a **WHICH?** question.

- If you want to know something about a person then ask a **WHO?** question.

- If you want to know the reason for something, then **WHY?** is for you.

- If you want to know if something is the right thing to do, then ask a **SHOULD?** question.

- Don't forget you can use **IS?** and **DOES?** too!

Once you have asked the questions, answering them will help you dig deeper.

How?

What?

When?

Where?

Which?

Why?

Is?

Who?

Does?

Should?

Truth-Seekers: **Thinking about Truth**

C10 In the eye of the beholder

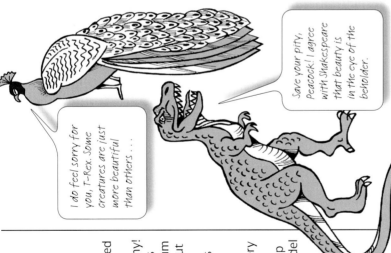

I do feel sorry for you, T-Rex. Some creatures are just more beautiful than others . . . .

Save your pity, Peacock! I agree with Shakespeare that beauty is in the eye of the beholder.

Merry was 22 months old. All the time she was discovering new things. One day she was in a shop when she saw something she liked immensely. She called out, 'Mummy! Look! Look! This is beautiful'. Her mum wandered over, but could not work out what Merry was referring to. She asked Merry if it was the flower painting that appeared so beautiful. Merry said, 'No'. She then asked her if it was the sparkly jewellery on the shelf that looked beautiful. Merry said, 'No'. Merry then pickec up a fierce, hard, and heavy looking model of a Tyrannasaurus Rex. She smiled at its sharp teeth and scaly skin. People around started to mutter, 'What does a lovely girl like that want with something so ugly?' Merry piped up, 'It is beautiful. Let's buy it! *Pleeease.*' While other toddlers went around cuddling dolls and teddy bears, Merry tucked in her dinosaur. Her mum thought about the sharp tail and the frightening face, but to Merry, nothing was lovelier.

What aspects of a dinosaur might be thought of as beautiful?

Why do you think Merry's mum did not think the dinosaur beautiful?

- Do you think that Merry was correct or mistaken about the dinosaur being beautiful?

- Who do you agree with, the peacock or the dinosaur? Explain your reasons.

- Brainstorm as many beautiful things as you can. Compare your list with another person's list.

- Underline the 10 most beautiful things in your list. Try to put them in order, with 1 being the most beautiful. Justify your choices.

- Share your list with other people. Do you disagree with any of the things that other people have listed as beautiful?

C13 What's at the heart?

Instructions

1 Brainstorm as many words as you can about the topic. Go for quantity and do not worry about quality for now. When you have as many words as possible, begin to sort them by how important they are.

2 Outside the ring, place words that are connected to your topic, but not that important.

3 In the outer ring place words that are quite important.

4 In the middle ring place words that are very important.

5 In the centre, place words that lie at the heart of the topic.

Connected, but not really important

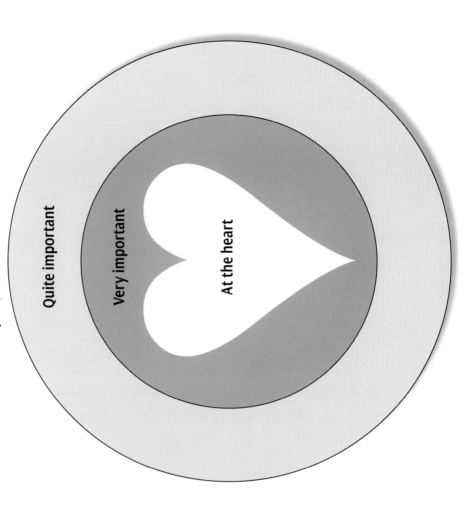

Quite important

Very important

At the heart

C12 Discovering truth

Look at this paragraph about Christian baptism from a textbook.

1.3 This is Baptism

Baptism is the entrance into the Christian Church. The person being baptised is either immersed in water in a pool, or is anointed on the head beside a font. A person is usually baptised with oil (chrism) or water. This physical act of baptism is accompanied by a set of promises. Baptism can be carried out at any age. Many Churches, such as the Church of England and the Catholic Church baptise people as infants. Other Churches, such as the Baptist Church, baptise believers when they reach an age where they are able to make a personal commitment for themselves. In the case of infant baptism, parents and godparents, on behalf of the child, make baptismal promises. A person usually takes on a Christian name when they are baptised. Many are names of Christian saints, such as John, Paul, Anne, Catherine.

All the information in this paragraph is factually correct. However, does this information really give us the truth about baptism?

If you wanted to discover what the truth about baptism you need to get to the heart of what baptism is.

- What people would you want to ask about baptism? Why?

- What questions would you want to ask these people about baptism?

- Why would you ask these questions?

- Is it possible to truly know something without experiencing it?

C14 The last days of Socrates

Socrates was a philosopher who lived 2500 years ago in Greece.

He was nicknamed 'The Gadfly'. A gadfly was a fly that had a sting. Socrates stung people into thinking about issues rather than blindly accepting them.

How far would you go to defend the truth?

Socrates was put on trial on two charges. The first charge was his refusal to accept the state religion. Socrates always looked to reason and his own conscience in decision-making.

The second charge was corruption of the young. Socrates was a teacher, but his methods were not traditional. He wanted his students to think for themselves. Socrates upset a lot of prominent people in Athens. He would expose speakers who sounded impressive, but in fact knew very little. Socrates was put on trial. The jury expected Socrates to deliver an elaborate defence, but he did not. Instead, he questioned the whole basis of the trial. By a very narrow margin, the Athenians found Socrates guilty. It was common for the accused and the accuser to suggest suitable punishments. One appropriate punishment would have been to accept exile to another part of Greece. Another suitable punishment would have been to give up discussing issues in public. Socrates did not suggest these punishments. He was committed to seeking truth and encouraging others to seek truth. Socrates suggested a small fine as a punishment. This was considered an insult. His prosecutor responded by asking for the death penalty. Death was by drinking hemlock (a poison). A large majority voted that Socrates be put to death.

Socrates' friends tried to persuade him to escape from jail and run away. With the help of his friend Crito, this could have been achieved. Socrates refused to do this on principle.

This dialogue is taken from Plato's book *Crito* (Plato was one of Socrates' students).

Socrates *Why have you come at this hour, Crito? It must be quite early.*

Crito Yes, certainly.

Socrates *What is the exact time?*

Crito The dawn is breaking.

Socrates *But you have not told me why you come at this early hour.*

Crito I come to bring you a message which is sad and painful; not, as I believe, to yourself but to all of us who are your friends, and saddest of all to me.

Socrates *What! I suppose that the ship has come from Delos, on the arrival of which I am to die?*

Crito No, the ship has not actually arrived, but she will probably be here today and therefore tomorrow, Socrates, will be the last day of your life. But, O! My beloved Socrates, let me entreat you once more to take my advice and escape. . . .

- What arguments might Crito have for asking Socrates to escape?
- What arguments might Socrates have for accepting his punishment?

C15 Truth and reconciliation

From 1948, South Africa was ruled by a government that had a policy of apartheid. This was a strict separation of races. The white-led government repressed the black population. Prominent black leaders, such as Nelson Mandela, were imprisoned. The government did not grant equal rights to black people. There was widespread violence and thousands of black people were killed. It was not until 1990 that Mandela was released and slowly systems of apartheid were taken apart. In 1994 the first democratic elections were held in South Africa, under Mandela as president, with people of all races being able to vote. Lots of black leaders called for the white officials responsible for apartheid acts to be punished in trials like the ones we have for war crimes. However, Mandela's government did not have trials for crimes under apartheid. They decided to establish the Truth and Reconciliation Commission instead.

The commission was responsible for investigating murders, unfair imprisonments and violence committed against black South Africans under apartheid. Individuals were blamed, but not punished. If an individual confessed his or her full role and showed that their actions were a result of a political policy, then they were given a reprieve and not punished.

The Truth and Reconciliation Commission was set up for a number of reasons. First, it was part of a compromise, which led to the end of apartheid. However, supporters maintained that this approach was more likely to end the cycle of violence in South Africa than punishments. If people were not afraid they would be imprisoned, then they would be more likely to come forward and accept blame for their crimes. This would help all South Africans to move on, as the perpetrators would take responsibility for their actions.

Nelson Mandela argued that truth is more important than justice. Once the truth of what happened during apartheid was openly acknowledged, then the country can move forward. Only once the country begins the move forward, can reconciliation and healing occur.

Imagine you were a black South African at the time apartheid ended.

1 What would you want to happen to the white officials responsible for acts of apartheid?

2 What would you say to Nelson Mandela when he set up the Truth and Reconciliation Commission?

3 Is truth more important than justice? Explain why or why not.

4 Is there another value that is more important than truth? Explain your answer.

C17 And if it's true?

And tonight the question on everybody's lips is, 'And is it true?' There are many who already believe and as many who remain unconvinced. However, by tomorrow morning we shall be certain once and for all. The truth will be out.

What impact will this news have on our lives and our ways of life? What changes will have to be made? Will this be the most important piece of knowledge in the history of our planet?

Come tomorrow, what will you be doing?

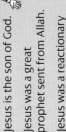

You have found out that the belief you hold most important has just been proven to the whole world. No longer is it a belief, but an irrefutable fact.

- You are a news reporter on the day that this 'truth' has been revealed to the world. Write a news report outlining how you think other people in the world will change as a result of the news.

1 You need to think about the beliefs that you hold and decide which one is most important to you.

2 Next, you need to think about how you would change your life if you could be sure that your belief was true.

3 You then need to think about how the lives of other people would alter if they knew the belief was true.

4 Think about whether the news would have a large or small impact on the way people live their lives now. Would there be knock-on consequences for the way people treat each other? On the policies governments make? On the way we educate children? On the things that we do socially? What about the effect it will have on other beliefs we currently hold?

C16 A deeper look at truth

Whose truth?

Look at the following statements:

Jesus is the son of God.

Jesus was a great prophet sent from Allah.

Jesus was a reactionary in the first century.

Jesus is the Way, the Truth and the Light.

Jesus died on the cross.

Jesus did not die on the cross, but was taken up to heaven by Allah.

- What steps (if any) can you take to discover which statements above are true?

- Is it important to discover the truth?

How important is the truth?

You are a Year 11 student taking nine GCSEs. In previous years, students from your school have not achieved very high GCSE grades. The local council will not give extra funding to your school unless exam grades improve. The teachers worry, as without extra funding they will not have enough money to help those students who do not do so well.

On the morning of your maths exam, you see some numbers up on the whiteboard. You realise that these are the answers to the exam. You cannot help looking.

When you get your grades in August, you receive an A for maths.

- Do you report the school? Why or why not?

How do we know we have the truth?

A long time ago, people thought that the earth was at the centre of the heavens. The sun and the moon were perfect. In biblical times, they believed that water surrounded the earth and entered as rain through windows in the atmosphere. Ptolemy, an astronomer in the second century, changed all this. He thought that the earth was at the centre of the universe and that the moon, the sun and the five known planets orbited it.

In 1530, a mathematician called Copernicus suggested that the earth orbited around the sun once yearly and the earth rotated around its own axis daily. He watched the skies from a cathedral tower. The first telescope had not even been invented. People thought this was an interesting mathematical idea, but did not think it true. In the early seventeenth century, a man named Galileo watched the stars with a home-made telescope. He saw the craters on the moon and the moon were not perfect. He saw that Copernicus was

right about cosmology. Despite opposition, Galileo declared Copernicus' ideas to be true.

In 1633, Galileo was put on trial for saying things that contradicted the established view. His theory was contrary to the literal meaning of the Bible. Galileo was placed under house arrest for the rest of his life and was forced to renounce his views.

- Why was it difficult for Galileo's views to be accepted?

- Have you ever believed something to be true, and then found out it was not true?

- If you were Galileo in 1630, how would you convince someone that your ideas were true?

People in the second century believed that they knew the truth about the universe. People in the seventeenth century who criticised Galileo thought that they knew the truth. Eventually all were proved wrong. His leaves us with a question: **How do we know that we have the truth?**

- Can we ever be sure that we have the truth? Explain your answers (with examples).

C18 Summary

Key words

Absolute

Accurate

Ambiguity

Belief

Clarity

Conflict

Depth

Fact

Lying

Opinion

Partial

Perspective

Pluralism

Postmodernism

Realist

Reasoned

Judgement

Relative

Tolerance

Truth

Truth claims

Understanding

Truth

Truth is important to us. We are expected to tell the truth in our jobs or at school. Knowing what the truth is enables us to make sensible choices.

Different religions claim that they have 'the truth'. These claims to truth often conflict.

Is there a truth to be found, or do we make truth ourselves?

Realism

Realists believe that the language that we use reflects reality. If Jemima claims that stealing is wrong, then realists will claim that there is a truth to be discovered. Either stealing is wrong, or it is right. Our language is trying to *correspond* to the state of affairs that is being described.

Postmodernism

Some people say there is no absolute truth. Postmodernists say that we make truths rather than discover them. The statement 'Stealing is wrong' might be true for our society as it fits in with all the other beliefs about how to live life. However, in the ancient Spartan society, stealing was regarded as a sign of bravery and cunning. Therefore, postmodernists will claim that we make truth.

Most religious people are realists. They believe that there is a truth to be discovered about God and their religion. However, some religious people are postmodernist. They believe that there are no truths to be found. They are happy to believe as long as the statement fits in with their way of life.

References

Unit A

p.8: *Meditations on First Philosophy*, René Descartes, (ed. John Cottingham), Cambridge University Press, 1996.

p.11: (A3) Confucius: *The Analects of Confucius: A Philosophical Translation*, Roger T. Ames, Ballantine Books, 1999; Sowell: *Knowledge and Decisions*, Thomas Sowell, Basic Books, 1996; Whitehead: *The Aims of Education*, A.N. Whitehead, The Free Press, 1967; King: *Strength to Love*, Martin Luther King, Fortress Press, 1981; Schopenhauer: *Studies in Pessimism*, A. Schopenhauer, http://ebooks.adelaide.edu.au/s/schopenhauer/arthur/pessimism; Durant: *The Story of Philosophy*, Will Durant, Touchstone books, 1999; da Vinci: source unknown; Einstein: source unknown; Seneca: *Naturales Quaestiones*, Seneca, trans. T.H. Corcoran, Loeb Classical Library, 1972; Bacon: source unknown; Goethe: source unknown; Wilde: *Intentions: The Critic as Artist*, Oscar Wilde, Unicorn Press, 1945; Einstein: source unknown; Aristotle: *Metaphysics*, Aristotle, trans. W.D. Ross, http://classics.mit.edu/Aristotle/metaphysics.2.ii.html; Hightower: source unknown; Socrates: *Protagoras and Meno*, Plato, Penguin Classics, 2005.

p.13: 'Is Justified True Belief Knowledge?', Edmund L. Gettier, *Analysis*, v.23, http://www3.sympatico.ca/saburns/pg0306b.htm.

p.18: *The Life of Samuel Johnson* (1791), James Bowell, Penguin Classics, 1979.

p.19: *Meditations on First Philosophy*, René Descartes; *Reason, Truth and History*, Hilary Putman, Cambridge University Press, 2008.

Unit B

p.30: *The Miniature Guide to Critical Thinking: Concepts and Tools*, Richard Paul, Linda Elder, Foundation for Critical Thinking, 2001; *Critical Thinking*, Brooke Moore, Richard Parker, McGraw Hill, 2006.

p.34: CNN/Time '2001' Global Influentials': www.time.com/time/2001/influentials.

p.39: *The Republic*, Plato, Penguin Classics, 2007.

Unit C

p.54: *Philosophers and Religious Truth*, Ninian Smart, Macmillan, 1970; *An Interpretation of Religion*, John Hick, Palgrave, 1994; *What is Truth?*, Peter Vardy, University of New South Wales Press, 2002; *Truth: A Guide for the Perplexed*, Simon Blackburn, Oxford University Press, 2007; *Why Truth Matters*, Jeremy Stangroom, Ophelia Benson, Continuum, 2006.

p.57: *Sophie's Choice*, William Styron, Vintage, 2004; *The Cruel Sea*, Nicholas Monsarrat, Penguin, 2002.

p.59: *Areopagitica: and Other Political Writings of John Milton*, John Milton, Liberty Fund Inc., 1999; *Collected Works, Vol 9: Aids to Reflection*, Samuel Taylor Coleridge, ed. John Beer, Princeton University Press, 1993.

p.61: *The Life of Pi*, Yann Martel, Canongate, 2003; *An Interpretation of Religion*, John Hick, Palgrave, 1994.

p.62: *Fear and Trembling*, Søren Kierkegaard, Penguin, 2005.

p.63: *Molly Bawn*, Margaret Wolfe Hungerford, Bastian Books, 2008.

p.67: *The Trial and Death of Socrates: Four Dialogues*, Plato, Dover Publications, 1992.

A **Truth-Seekers: Thinking about Truth** CD-ROM is included with this book.

Important

Inspection copies of this CD may be previewed by schools subject to the following conditions:

- The CD remains the property of the publisher until paid for in full and **must not** be copied, stored or downloaded to a computer **in any way**.
- The plastic CD wallet must not be detached from the book cover.
- If you decide not to purchase this resource, the CD must be replaced in the wallet and returned to RMEP with the book in mint condition within 30 days of receipt (postage paid by you), otherwise you will be charged the full invoiced price (including VAT).